Bringing the Stars down to Earth

So you know your sign, you've read your horoscope in the newspaper and magazines, heard all about how Geminis are great with Leos but can't get along with Virgos, and seen all those tabloid predictions. Now you're wondering, "Is that all there is to astrology?"

Well, actually, it's just the beginning. *What Astrology Can Do for You* opens the door to the real purpose and power of astrology—understanding yourself, your path, and your future.

People are as unique as snowflakes, and, as you learn about all the elements that go into your one-of-a-kind birth chart, you will be taking your first steps on a lifelong journey to the stars.

About the Author

A professional astrologer for twenty-five years, Stephanie Jean Clement, Ph.D., has been a board member of the American Federation of Astrologers since 1991. She has lectured and given workshops in the United States and Canada on psychological counseling and astrology. Stephanie's published books include *Charting Your Career: The Horoscope Reveals Your Life Purpose*; *Decanates and Dwads*; *Counseling Techniques in Astrology*; and *Planets and Planet-Centered Astrology*. In addition, she has published numerous articles on astrological counseling, charts of events, and counseling techniques.

To Write to the Author

If you wish to contact the author or would like more information about this book, please write to the author in care of Llewellyn Worldwide, and we will forward your request. Both the author and publisher appreciate hearing from you and learning of your enjoyment of this book and how it has helped you. Llewellyn Worldwide cannot guarantee that every letter written to the author can be answered, but all will be forwarded. Please write to:

Stephanie Jean Clement
c/o Llewellyn Worldwide Ltd.
P.O. Box 64383, Dept. K146–5
St. Paul, MN 55164–0383, U.S.A.

Please enclose a self-addressed, stamped envelope for a reply or $1.00 to cover costs. If outside the U.S.A., enclose international postal reply coupon.

What Astrology Can Do for You

STEPHANIE JEAN CLEMENT, PH.D.

2000
Llewellyn Publications
St. Paul, Minnesota, 55164–0383 U.S.A.

FIRST EDITION
First Printing, 2000

Cover design by William Merlin Cannon
Interior design and editing by Eila Savela

All horoscope charts in this book were generated using Winstar © Matrix Software.

Library of Congress Cataloging-in-Publication Data
Clement, Stephanie Jean.
    What astrology can do for you / Stephanie Jean Clement.--1st ed.
        p. cm.
    ISBN 1–56718–146–
    1. Astrology.   I. Title

BF 1708.1.C54 2000
133.5--dc21   99–049041
                                                         CIP

Llewellyn Publications
A Division of Llewellyn Worldwide, Ltd.
P.O. Box 64383, Dept. Dept. K146–5
St. Paul, Minnesota, 55164–0383, U.S.A.
www.llewellyn.com

 Printed in the United States of America on recycled paper

Other Books by
Stephanie Jean Clement

Counseling Techniques in Astrology
(American Federation of Astrologers)

Decanates and Dwads
(American Federation of Astrologers)

Planets and Planet-Centered Astrology
(American Federation of Astrologers)

Charting Your Career
(Llewellyn Publications)

Contents

Contents

Contents

Illustrations

Chapter One

Welcome to the World of Astrology

Your astrological chart (sometimes called the *horoscope*) contains a wealth of information about you and about every area of your life. With it you will discover information about yourself, and you will confirm ideas or feelings that may have been floating just out of reach. At first, the chart may seem like a circle filled with numbers and foreign symbols, but as you read this little book, you will find that the symbols become more familiar, and their meanings begin to make sense. Throughout the book you will find frequently asked questions printed in italic type. These questions are listed in the table of contents for your convenience.

It seems that people have always been fascinated by the stars. As a child you may have spent an evening lying in the grass, looking up at the sky. You probably discovered the patterns of a few constellations—perhaps the Big and Little Dippers or the Belt of Orion or the *W* of Cassiopeia. And you discovered, perhaps, that they look different at different times of the year, or different times of the night. Sometimes that *W* looks a lot more like an *M*.

What is astrology, exactly?

Astrology is an organized system of information about the stars and how they reflect our earthly reality. Your chart is a map of the positions of the planets, the Sun, and the Moon amid the background of the constellations or signs of the zodiac. When astrology began, the constellations and the signs were aligned with each other. Due to the gravitational force of the Sun and Moon upon Earth, the point in the sky we define as the spring equinox has moved backward through the zodiac. This is called *precession*, and the movement has resulted in the equinox moving backward through Pisces to the sign of Aquarius. This is what is meant by the term Age of Aquarius—the Sun now rises in the part of the zodiac we call Aquarius at the time of the spring equinox.

Because the spring equinox is tied to the season of the year, and because Western astrology has defined the signs in terms of the seasons, we define the sign Aries as both the beginning of the zodiac and the beginning of the spring season. Therefore, zero degrees of Aries is the point in the heavens the Sun occupies at the spring equinox. All of the signs are defined as equal segments of the circle, with Libra at the fall equinox, and with Cancer and Capricorn at the summer and winter solstices.

Why do I need to know my birth time?

Your chart is a map of the planets as they relate to those segments of the circle. Using mathematical calculations, the astrologer (or a computer program) begins with your birth date, place, and time. The first thing is to determine what part of the sky was highest in the sky when you were born. This point is called the Midheaven, and in most charts it is at the top of the page. Imagine yourself standing at your birthplace, facing south (or north if you were born in the Southern Hemisphere). As you look up in the sky, you can imagine particular stars, among them the planets that were "up" at the time you were born. If you were born during the day, of course, you would only be able to see the Sun, and possibly the Moon. Nonetheless, the background of stars and planets is there.

Astrological calculations determine the exact point of the Midheaven first. From there the Ascendant or rising sign is calculated. On your chart this is the point on the left side of the circle. It represents the part of the zodiac that was rising in the east at your birth time and place. If you are at your birth place and look east to the place where the Sun would rise, that is where the Ascendant is located. Depending on the time of year, this point may be somewhat further north or south, but it is always generally east of the birth place.

What if I don't know my birth time?

By now you are beginning to understand why the exact time and place of birth are significant. The Midheaven and Ascendant depend on this information. The more accurate the information, the more precise your chart becomes, and the more accurate the interpretation of the astrologer. If you don't know your birth time, you can ask family members or look on your birth certificate (the official one). If you cannot obtain a birth time, you can still learn a great deal about yourself through astrology. You can use a chart with the Sun on the Ascendant (this is called a *sun rising chart* and is set for about 6:00 in the morning, a very common birth time). Your astrologer may recommend using a birth time of noon (thereby choosing planetary placements from the middle of the day). In either of these charts, the Midheaven and Ascendant are not accurate, but astrologers find that the houses themselves may prove to make a lot of sense.

If you are consulting an astrologer, he or she may ask you some questions about your life experiences and when they occurred, and can then estimate (or rectify) your birth time. One whole phase of a professional astrologer's studies is directed toward this kind of work.

How do I read my chart?

The next step is to divide the chart into twelve sections, called houses. While the signs represent different facets of collective life, and different expressions of life's energy, the houses represent different areas of your personal life. The signs are the same for everyone, but the houses are unique to your chart, as they are based on your time and place of birth. The twelve houses, discussed more fully in chapter 7, cover everything from your personality to how you relate to other people's resources, from your home to your work environment, from your creative endeavors to travel. Every human experience fits into the chart—astrology is a reflection of every thing you think, feel, or do. By understanding the chart you can gain insight into areas of your life that are troublesome or unclear. You can also maximize your potential by discovering where the flow is

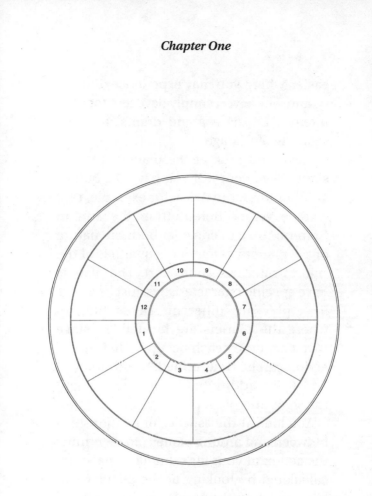

Figure 1. Astrological Wheel.

easier, where you may experience difficulty, and where you simply have less focused interest. Life is a grand drama, and the signs are life's stage.

Next, you look at the planets and the signs they occupy. If you have the Sun or another planet in Aries, for example, that will be very different from the Sun in Gemini. You can consider both the nature of the planet itself and the qualities of the sign to interpret your chart. The planets have specific characteristics, just as actors in a play are different. Depending on where the planets are located on stage (what sign they each occupy), their interaction can be determined. See chapters 5 and 6 for additional information about the signs and planets.

You look at the aspects, or relationships between and among planets, to determine the action of your life's drama. Aspects are calculated by looking at the angular distance between the planets, or how far apart they are on the chart's circle. Certain distances are more significant than others, and those are the aspects that are considered. Aspects are discussed in chapter 8.

These basic considerations are based on a foundation of many centuries of study. Because the planets, signs, houses, and aspects are so consistent, it has been possible to develop computer reports that cover all the basics of chart interpretation. The personal services offered at the end of this book are based on the finest calculations available, coupled with interpretations written by highly qualified astrologers. (See the appendix for a list of services available through Llewellyn Worldwide.) In fact, many professional astrologers supplement their personal consultations with printed reports about the birth chart and about the current time period. These serve as a basic interpretation of your birth chart and as a general guide for the coming months that you can refer to from time to time.

Now that we have this overview, let's look at what astrology is and what it can do in more detail.

Chapter Two

How Astrology Is Different from Psychic Prediction

Astrology is a science, based upon the mathematical calculation of the planets' positions in the sky, and their relationships to each other and to the Ascendant and Midheaven. By using the longitude of your birth place, the date, and the time, an astrologer computes the exact part of the zodiac that was highest in the sky when you were born. This is the Midheaven. Then, using the latitude of the place you were born, the Ascendant, or rising sign, is calculated. This results in a chart that is unique to you. Even twins have small differences between their charts as a result of the time difference.

Once an astrologer has created your horoscope, or birth chart, then they use time-tested and proven data about the planets and their relationships (called aspects) to interpret the chart. You could compare this process to using a map when you are travelling. The map is not the territory, but it is a representation of where the roads, towns, and geographic features are in relation to each other. Your birth chart is not you, but it is a very accurate representation of your potential in every area of your life. It is a reflection of what the larger universe looked like at the time you were born. Astrology uses this reflection, or map, to tell you about yourself and your best, most creative potential.

Astrologers also move the planets forward in time to the present or other significant dates in order to compare those placements to the birth chart. Different methods are used to move the planets ahead. One is symbolic (*progressions*) and the other is the actual placement of the planets on the date being considered (*transits*). The symbolic movement is based on tried and true methods of determining the individual psychological or emotional tone of a moment, while the transits are used to indicate astrological influences that everyone has in common on that date. The three factors—birth chart, progressions, and transits—are then compared and interpreted, producing a forecast.

Astrologers do not produce the forecast from psychic impressions. Rather they use what they have learned from studies of past events. This is a bit like reading x-rays in a doctor's office. The x-ray is a picture of something that we cannot see with our eyes. Through experience the doctor learns what the shadows on the film mean. Astrologers rely on similar historical experience accumulated and recorded over a period of centuries.

Once the astrologer has examined the charts, interpretations are made based on what they know about the client. It is important for the astrologer to know your physical capabilities, your social situation, where you were raised, and even your educational level. The chart for your birth time could be a chart for anyone or anything born at that time and place, so the context of your life is a very important factor in producing an accurate interpretation of how you will respond to the energies pictured in the charts.

Psychics depend on their inner sense of what is happening around them. They have a sixth sense. Actually, everyone has some of this ability. You may have had experiences that are psychic in nature, such as times when you hear the phone ring and know who it is before you answer. You may have felt that something was about to happen, and then it did. These incidents are examples of what psychics use to tell you about yourself.

Most psychics use tools to aid their psychic ability. They may have crystals, cards, geomancy tools, or other tools. These are used to focus the psychic ability when they want to learn about you and your situation. Psychics also depend on what they know of your actual situation. Some people feel that psychics use contextual information to "make up" their readings—that they simply take what they know about you and fantasize about what is a likely outcome. I am of the opinion that many psychics are using abilities that we all have, and that they have developed these abilities beyond the average level. I also feel that a psychic can miss the mark because of personal issues. The astrologer has the advantage of being able to rely on proven data.

The fact that astrologers have a body of data available is the reason that computerized astrology reports are useful. The data can be recorded in a computer program and then applied to your personal chart. Such a report does not include the context of your life at the present moment, but it does analyze the astrological information. It can be as complete as the programmer can make it, but you must supply the context. Generally, you will read such an astrological interpretation and find that a lot of it applies to your situation, and that some of it either does not seem to apply at all or is not important at that time. The interpretation gives you information to ponder—surprises in the report may make you think about yourself in a different light or provide the chance to consider a course of action that you had not been aware of before.

A computerized report is like the results of blood work in a doctor's office. The numbers come back—you have a certain level of cholesterol, or some mineral seems to be lacking. The doctor uses the report and what is known about you personally to recommend a course of treatment. Astrologers use the computer both to produce the birth chart and related charts, and to produce written interpretations. Or they use the charts and do the interpretation themselves. Then they apply what they see in the chart to what they know about your situation.

Perhaps you have asked a question concerning a possible career change. You can obtain a career report from a computer. It will contain information about your natural aptitudes, as seen in your birth chart, and also information about the current situation. This report will focus on the part of the chart that relates to career issues. When you read your career report, you can supply the contextual information yourself in many cases. You know, for instance, about your physical capabilities. If the report mentions a sport in which you have no particular skill, for example, you can give that less emphasis, and instead concentrate on another option where you have interest and skills.

The astrologer may see information in your chart that has little to do with career, but will focus on the parts of the chart that relate to your career question. They will also give advice concerning unrelated areas, if they feel those areas will affect the process of your proposed career change. I sometimes ask questions about things in a chart that catch my interest, even if they seem to have little bearing on the question I have been asked to explore, much the way a psychic would converse during a psychic reading, gathering information about how the reading relates to your situation.

Both psychics and astrologers are likely to connect with you in some areas, and both are likely to provide information that does not relate in any obvious way. To the extent that an astrologer can explore your chart without comparing it to other people, the reading will be clearly about you. To the extent a psychic can sort out psychic input and filter out information that does not relate to you personally, the reading will be clearly about you. Astrologers have the advantage of a solid factual basis for their interpretations, and depend far less on personal psychic clarity for their interpretations. Thus, an astrological reading is more dependable.

Chapter Three

How Astrology Can Work for You

Aside from this birth chart, what can astrology do for me?

Astrologers use the birth chart and other calculations to consider every kind of question imaginable. The most frequently asked questions are about romance or finance and career: *When will I marry? Will this relationship last? Will this business deal work out? When? What is in store for me next year?* Astrologers also use charts to answer such questions as: *Where is my lost necklace? Who will win the Super Bowl?* A few astrologers are having better success predicting the weather than the weatherman, and much further in advance!

You might read books or obtain a computer-generated interpretation for specific reasons:

- to learn more about yourself— your strengths and challenges;

- to understand and overcome limitations;

- to explore your dreams and how they fit into your life;

- to compare your chart to another person to see how well you will get along;

- to determine careers that are most appropriate to your birth chart, and to the stage of your life at the present time;

- to answer medical questions;

- to find lost objects or answer other very specific questions;

- to forecast trends for the coming six months or year;

- to select a place to live (geographical location);

- to learn about your spiritual development and mission;

- to relate to your children better; and

- to gain understanding about anything that arises in your life, and to deal with transitions more effectively.

What else? The stars are the limit—they provide limitless potential.

I'm just a beginner. Can you recommend a very basic book for me?

There are many books on the market, so this is a good question to ask yourself. At the end of this volume, you can order Llewellyn's publication *New Worlds*. In *New Worlds* you will find titles that are for beginners. They don't assume that you know a lot of information, and they go through the material step by step. Some of these titles have sold over 100,000 copies worldwide and have been translated into many languages. They are written by professional astrologers who have studied their craft, and whom we feel are interesting writers, as well.

Do I have to learn all that math to do astrology?

No, you don't. Before the age of computers, astrologers had to calculate every detail of the chart. Now you can find reasonably priced computer programs that will do the calculations, or you can get charts through astrological service providers.

It is important for you to learn enough about how charts are calculated to know if you are looking at an accurate chart. Here are some pointers:

- Is the Sun in the right part of the chart for the time of day? The chart resembles a clock, but for a twenty-four hour time period. The top of the chart is noon, the left side is about 6:00 A.M., the right side about 6:00 P.M., and the bottom is midnight. The Sun should appear in the approximate part of the chart for the time of day—3:00 P.M. is in the upper right-hand section of the chart. Daylight saving time or war time will affect the placement to some extent, but this is a good rule of thumb.

- Are the outer planets in the right signs for the year you are looking at? The outer planets move slowly. Pluto can be in the same sign for as long as thirty years. Saturn takes about twenty-eight to thirty years to go through the signs. You can expect all the charts for several years to have the outer planets in the same signs, and you can check these placements in tables, or compare charts to see if they are close to the same.

- Does the printout tell you the date, time, and place that were used to calculate the chart? Is that information correct? If the printout does not contain this information, then you may want to obtain a chart that does. If the information is correct, then you can figure the chart is correct. This, of course, assumes that you have a good quality program, based on accurate mathematics.

How do I decide if I want to learn astrology?

We recommend that you try one book or book with a CD-ROM program. You probably don't want to invest in a complete library of astrology books at first, but you can start with a beginner's book. If the material fascinates you—if you want to get the charts of all your friends and family and examine them—then you have the makings of a future astrologer. If you are really more interested in your own chart, you still may want to get other books on specific subjects. Astrology is a valuable self-education tool, too!

Chapter Four

A Lottery Winner

The example chart is for a woman (let's call her Jane) who purchased a lottery ticket on February 5, 1998, got into a legal battle with the store owner where she purchased it, and settled the case on August 7, 1998, with Jane declared as the winner.

Can astrology predict "lucky" periods in life?

There isn't space to interpret every area of Jane's life in this little book. However, we can highlight indications of luck in her chart, and also describe what was happening during 1998. Jane has the Sun in Libra in the Second House. The Libra Sun indicates her general sociable approach to life, and reflects her tendency to seek harmony in her surroundings and relationships. Associations with other people are important to her. With the Sun in the Second House, money matters are important to Jane. Her practical nature has helped her to create a comfortable life that is stable, for the most part. The basic point here is that money and material things play a significant role in her life.

The Virgo Ascendant indicates that Jane is thorough and careful, and that she pays attention to the details of her life. She may be fussy about things, or possibly just careful where details are concerned. She may prefer simple but elegant clothing and jewelry.

The Gemini Midheaven reflects the fact that Jane understands her own capacity to scatter her energies. She is a thinker, and her daily life is filled with thoughts, sometimes focused, sometimes random. She knows that harnessing her thinking ability is key to her success. She is happiest in a career that puts her in direct communication with others, and it is this skill that is essential to her success. Here, creativity comes in spurts.

Jane
October 16, 1925

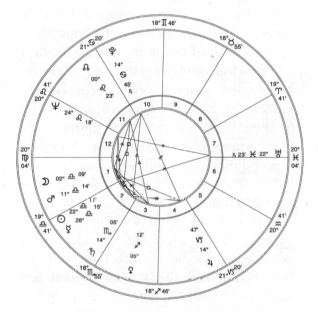

Geocentric
Tropical
Koch Houses

Figure 2. Jane's Natal Chart.

The Moon in Libra supports the Sun by bringing expressed individuality into harmonious balance with her inner subconscious life. She needs love in her life and seeks a compatible partner. At the same time she finds herself overemphasizing things that are really not very important. There is a lot of flux in her dream life and subconscious, and this is sometimes reflected outwardly as inconsistency in her behavior. She may be self-indulgent in some ways.

There are two striking patterns of aspects in the chart. Patterns are important because they show different kinds of energy that can be easily used together, thus strengthening one's abilities. Jane has Saturn, Uranus, and Pluto forming a triangle called a Grand Trine. The Grand Trine is considered to be a fortunate pattern because it reflects the fact that Jane can use several different kinds of energy together smoothly. The energies in this case are basically personal power and will (Pluto), intuition (Uranus), and awareness of structure and intelligent activity (Saturn).

Jane
October 16, 1925

Outer Ring
lottery ticket trans
February 5, 1998

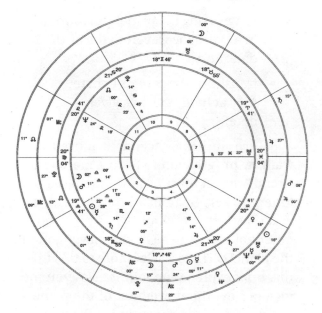

Middle Ring
lottery ticket dir
February 5, 1998

Geocentric
Tropical
Koch Houses

Figure 3. Jane's Directed and Transit Chart.

This pattern is not exact, but it becomes more exact at the time she purchased her lottery ticket. How does it become more exact? Astrologers use two general methods of forecasting:

- progressing the planets forward in a symbolic way from the birth date, and

- transits of the planets (where they actually are on a given date).

Saturn and the Ascendant moved forward by progression to form a more exact Grand Trine at the time Jane purchased her lottery ticket. By transit Jupiter makes an exact aspect to Pluto. Thus, the birth potential is enhanced by the movement of the planets. There is a lot more to this than this brief explanation, but it gives you the idea of how the movement of the planets affects the birth chart and reflects your changing focus and fortune in life.

She also has the Sun, Uranus, and Neptune forming a triangle called a Yod. This pattern is indicative of her psychic (Neptune) and intuitive (Uranus) ability, and how they relate to her personal (Sun in Libra in the Second House) approach to money and material matters. The Sun moved by progression to form a positive aspect with Uranus, thus enhancing Jane's psychic and intuitive senses.

Can astrology predict a lottery winner?

Could Jane have predicted that she would win? Probably not, but a good astrologer could have recognized the enhanced patterns and suggested that Jane focus on her intuition and psychic abilities, that she listen to her heart or pay attention to the messages from her inner guides. Because of the nature of the aspects in the patterns, astrology would also have been able to forecast some adjustments in Jane's life, specifically where money and material matters are concerned. Other aspects suggest that seeking advice from competent associates (like a lawyer) may be a good idea.

What can I forecast using astrology?

Once you understand your birth chart and the potentials reflected there, you can use the progressions and transits to forecast trends of energy in your life. You can relate your daily, monthly, and yearly activities to the cycles of the planets as they move through aspects. When two or more cycles converge, there is a higher probability of certain kinds of events, and certainly the psychological shifts that the planets suggest. It is because of the pressure of energy that we decide to make changes. The planets reflect the kind of energy that is producing the pressure, but they are not the decision-making mechanism.

It's a bit like driving a car. When you see a curve in the road, you adjust your steering. When you are on an uphill stretch, you engage the accelerator, and when you are on a downhill section you apply the brakes. When the road is wide and straight, you sail ahead. Astrology shows you the metaphorical curves and bumps in the road of life so that you can plan around them.

Chapter Five

The Signs of
the Zodiac

What is the zodiac?

The signs of the zodiac are the most widely known part of the astrological system. As mentioned earlier, almost everyone knows their Sun sign. The daily horoscopes in the newspaper are based on the position of the Sun in the zodiac. The zodiac is made up of twelve signs, defined as equal segments of the circle. Each sign contains thirty degrees. The path of the plants around the Sun follows a circle described by the zodiac. From our point of view on Earth, it is the Sun that moves through the signs.

How do I figure out my sign?

The birth date determines the Sun sign. With some slight variations caused by leap years and by the fact that the year is not exactly 360 days, the Sun is in the same part of the zodiac at the same time each year. The exact time and date when the Sun moves from one sign to the next varies, and if you are born around the "cusp," you will need to get an exact chart cast to determine your sign.

What is a cusp?

The word cusp means point. It is the point of transition from one astrological sign to another, or from one historical period to the next. A cusp is a turning point. The transition from one sign to the next occurs at a specified moment. On the personal level this change is felt over an extended period of time, so that even though you may have been born at the end of one sign, you may feel the energy of the next sign very strongly. Therefore you may have the character traits of both signs to a certain extent.

Each astrological chart contains all twelve signs, and the planets are spread through the signs in a pattern based on their positions in the sky at a given time. You will not have a planet in every sign, and some people have numerous planets in one sign. The signs color or modify the energy of the planets. The Sun in each sign reflects the energy of that sign, and the same is true of the Moon and planets. The energy of Mars will be expressed differently in Aries than in Gemini. To understand how a planet works, you can first read the information about the planet, and think of that as the actor. Then read the section about the sign, and think of that as the stage setting. The energetic, argumentative Mars character will physically move more forcefully in Aries, will try to communicate more forcefully in Gemini, and will pay more attention to details when in Virgo.

What about empty signs?

Just because you have empty signs in your chart, that does not mean those signs are not part of your life. As the planets move through the sky and the signs, they bring those energies into your life. The constantly changing pattern is a reflection of the changes in your thoughts and feelings, and in the events in your life. During the year you experience the Sun in every sign. During your life you will experience the seven visible planets (out to Saturn) in every sign, and the invisible planets (Uranus, Neptune, and Pluto) in several or more signs. Pluto, for example, requires 247 years to revolve around the Sun, so you will only experience Pluto in a few signs during one lifetime.

How can I figure out where the planets are now?

There are three basic ways to do this:

- Look at a star map. Astrologers use the same symbols as astronomers, so you can see the signs defined along the ecliptic (the path of Earth around the Sun), and the planets are positioned around the circle. Star charts are published in many newspapers and magazines for each month.

- Look at an ephemeris. An ephemeris is a listing of the positions of the Sun, Moon, and planets, usually for each day. Astrology uses these lists to calculate birth charts. They also look at the ephemeris to see where the plants are on a particular day, and compare those positions to the birth chart. The current positions of the planets are called transits.

- Obtain an astrological chart that is set for today. This chart is a birth chart for the current time. You can also get a chart that has your birth planets in one circle and the transits in an outer circle, so that you can easily see where the transits are in relation to your own chart.

Tell me something about each of the signs.

The following section describes each of the signs. You will find that you relate more easily to some signs than others. This may be because you have planets in those signs in your birth chart. Another reason is that certain signs are more compatible with others. This compatibility is based on two main relationships: elements and modes.

- The elements are organized into four groups: fire, earth, air, and water. Each sign is very compatible with other signs of the same element, somewhat compatible with the opposite element (fire and air, or earth and water), and less compatible with the remaining two elements.

- The modes are qualities of expression (cardinal or active, fixed or steady, and mutable or changeable). Generally signs of the same mode relate to each other most easily.

Fire: Aries, Leo, Sagittarius
*Spiritual, active, creative, and coura-
geous*

Earth: Capricorn, Taurus, Virgo
Physical, reserved, and industrious

Air: Libra, Aquarius, Gemini
Mental, observant, and expressive

Water: Cancer, Scorpio, Pisces
Emotional, imaginative, and psychic

**Cardinal: Aries, Cancer, Libra,
Capricorn**
Pioneering and expressive

Fixed: Taurus, Leo, Scorpio, Aquarius
Stable and persistent

**Mutable: Gemini, Virgo, Sagittarius,
Pisces**
Adaptable and changeable

What signs am I most compatible with?

Generally, you are more compatible with
the same or opposite elements. However,
remember there are nine other planets to

consider besides the Sun, and compatibility depends on those placements as well. Thus, an Aries and a Cancer, while not so compatible by Sun sign, may find that they get along well because the Aries has the Moon and the Ascendant in Cancer, while the Cancer has them in Aries, thereby establishing strong links. Plus, Aries and Cancer are both cardinal signs, so they share a general tendency toward action.

As you read the following descriptions of the signs, notice the signs that are the same element or mode, and you will see some of the shared characteristics and tendencies. The descriptions of the signs will include:

- personality (what people see in you),

- mentality (how your mind works, but not intelligence per se),

- temperament (how you express yourself), and

- disposition (how you respond to other people).

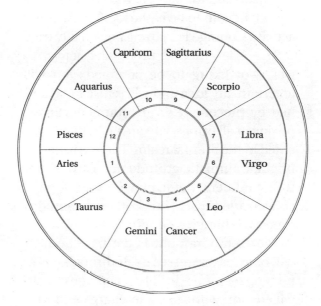

Figure 4. Astrological Signs.

Aries

The best quality of Aries is leadership. The worst quality is officiousness. A key phrase is "I am." The Aries personality is energetic and ambitious. You want to be in command and to be in the forefront of every activity. Courage is a strong personality trait.

The Aries mental process is active, as well. Not liking to be confined, you will entertain any idea and will refuse to be limited by precedent or environment. Enterprising in all things, you are no less goal-oriented in the mental realm. There is usually a bright, optimistic attitude that carries over to a confident demeanor. You are a good conversationalist, but others shouldn't expect to change your mind.

Your temperament is daring. The fiery will of Aries expresses itself through forceful engagement in life's activities. Self-willed, you want to be in charge and may not take instruction well. Independent and impulsive, Aries can be rash at times. The desire to be ahead of others often leads to a competitive demeanor.

As mentioned above, the thought processes and temperament often lead

Aries to be combative, or at the very least assertive. You would make a good executive because you have the drive to get ahead. Still, your headlong rush into things can be less than inspired at times. A keen mental edge and incisive wit make Aries interesting to be with, but tiresome when wit turns to sarcasm and mental activity becomes obsessive.

So, why is a potentially obsessive or sarcastic individual a good leader? Because beneath these possibilities lies the resourcefulness to try something different in order to make a difference. Like the ram, you see a target, put your head down, and charge. After the initial thrust, you look around, reset your direction and charge again. Enthusiasm is contagious, and you can be the source of it. Self-reliance and enterprise are traits we admire in leaders, because we know that you will be able to manage in difficult circumstances. Just as you demand your own personal freedom, you recognize that others need personal space, too. Aries' color is red. Your part of the body is the head.

Taurus

☿ The best quality of Taurus is stability. The worst quality is stubbornness. A key phrase is "I have." The Taurean personality is industrious, sometimes even plodding. It is easy to imagine a Taurus still going, like the Energizer Bunny, when everyone else has quit for the day. Once you get on a roll, you don't want to stop. You have enormous energy reserves. You can pursue a single task for a long time, but then switch tracks and take on another task. You may not know when to rest.

Taurus is seen as being reliable and, generally, consistent. Taurus is immovable. Once you have made up your mind, changing it is like moving a mountain. You may listen to the opinions of others, but then stick to your own. You are interested in the psychic realm, because it is so close to the present moment.

You know the value of money and appreciate material possessions. The Taurean mentality leans toward practical things. Generally careful, you can discriminate quality and tend to be a perfectionist.

Conservative in temperament, you appreciate the traditional way of doing things. You are unlikely to abandon a system just because it has a flaw—you are more likely to capitalize on its strengths and find a way around the problem.

Taurus is patient. You can wait for the right time to act, and allow others the time they need to accomplish their tasks—that is only practical, after all! Taurus enjoys a daily routine, a weekly routine, even an annual routine. Generally, you cannot be rushed into action. You are like a train—you only move as fast as you move. Yet Taurus is usually efficient, not wanting to waste effort, thereby discovering the most direct path.

Taurus tends toward a reserved disposition. You dislike change and are, therefore, less likely to force change on others. You are possessive and, as a result, do not demand that others give up their possessions. Taurus, like the bull, is placid and willing to take whatever comes, as long as it doesn't irritate overmuch. Taurus' colors are pastels, especially pinks and blues. The parts of the body are the throat and lower jaw.

Chapter Five

Gemini

Ⅱ Gemini's best quality is versatility. The worst quality is changeableness. A key phrase is "I think." As a mutable sign, Gemini is changeable, and this can be the best or worst of qualities.

Your versatility allows you to learn a little about just about everything and to develop skills in many areas. This makes for a good executive or manager, because you are able to oversee multiple activities and keep track of many projects at once. Other people can almost see the wheels turning. Gemini appears to be open-minded. Yet, a time comes when no more oddball ideas can be wedged into the system. Then Gemini draws upon skillful thought processes to decide what to keep and what to discard.

Gemini is a mental sign, often intellectually driven. The capacity for communication includes both listening and speaking, making Gemini a wonderful companion and writer. Where Taurus wants physical expression, Gemini seeks out mentally challenging activities. You enjoy the learning process. Gemini is intuitive, and are able to see into the future and gauge the results of actions—another worthy executive trait.

Gemini's temperament is volatile in the true meaning of this term. You can vaporize at a relatively low temperature, and you seem to be able to fly. Some people see this as the fickleness of a butterfly flitting from one flower to the next. The strength is in the ability to rise above the pettiness of situations to see the larger picture. Your mantra might be, "It just doesn't matter." Gemini is dexterous of hand, eye, and wit, with the ability to turn a situation or conversation in a new direction at will.

In spite of this sign's apparent adaptability, Gemini is sensitive at heart. You are aware of what others are thinking and feeling, and often take a diplomatic path to avoid hurting others. This could be at your own expense, although you don't let us know it. Tolerance should not be mistaken for a lack of emotional depth. Gemini's parts of the body are the arms and lungs. Monochromatic or bright colors are best.

Cancer

♋ The best quality of Cancer is the ability to nurture the self and others. The worst quality is holding on to things too tightly. A key phrase is "I feel."

The Cancerian personality is family and home oriented. The emotional well-being of the home environment is key to Cancer's emotional balance, which is even-tempered when it flows. When opposed, the Cancerian temperament can display other water characteristics, like freezing or flood stage emotions. Never let the emotional side of Cancer fool you into thinking you are not leaders—this sign provides leadership in the feeling arena and can be influential in all areas where subjective feelings are important.

The Cancerian mind will often ask "how does this feel?" before deciding what action to take. You are true to your belief system and it may be difficult to steer into any activity you cannot support on the "gut" level. This attention to inner feelings puts you in a good position in industries that appeal to the mass market, as you don't lose sight of individual preferences in the pursuit of the big picture.

Cancer is a water sign. Water takes the shape of the vessel that contains it, and water runs downhill. The Cancer temperament will go with the flow when that is convenient, and can be quite happy if the vocational, relationship, or recreational container suits the individual. Sometimes you surprise people, though, when you resist going a certain direction "on principle." Stick to those principles, as they set you apart from people who either don't seem to know what they really believe, or are not able to hold your ground in the face of opposition.

Generally, you respond to others in a caring or nurturing context. You may consider what will help move a process along, or you decide what people should wear or eat, based on their needs, not yours. At the same time, you can be a skillful manager, helping others to map out a clear, well-defined process for your activities. You are good at keeping projects on track—you know how to find the strongest current in the river, and then keep your craft headed into that current. The breasts and stomach fall under Cancer's rulership. Cancer's color is violet.

Leo

The best quality of Leo is kindness. The worst quality is domination. A key phrase is "I lead." Leo's personality is strong, even majestic. Leo wants to be dignified in every situation, and also may want to dominate. Stability is a pronounced trait.

The mental process tends toward large ideas. Leo is determined to rise to a position of authority and despises petty tasks. The desire for personal glory sometimes leads Leo's reach to exceed the grasp in the pursuit of honors or high office. The individual will is generally focused, and cannot be easily swayed.

Your passionate temperament makes you exciting to be around. You can be entertaining, as you seek the limelight, if not the love of the audience. You act from emotion or intuition, and may fail to consider the price of your actions. Impulsive and daring, you make a good leader, determined to win. You can also be willful, holding your own position in spite of the wisdom of the alternative.

The Leo disposition is sympathetic and warm-hearted for the most part. In leadership situations these qualities may manifest in the fact that you do not demand the impossible of others—that you reserve for yourself. Once committed, you are faithful and trust in others. You are not very good at taking orders.

You are a fair opponent. You recognize a good challenge and bring courage and nobility to the battle. Your persistence in the pursuit of your goals can provide leadership in difficult situations where others might quit. Like the lion, you wish to dominate your surroundings, but are willing to bask in the Sun in a dignified manner. Once you have made a decision, you are outspoken in the expression of your position. You can be overbearing when you determine to get your own way. It is better to seek your agreement than to try to force you to accept someone else's views. Leo rules the heart. The best colors for Leo are orange and gold.

Virgo

♍ The best quality of Virgo is analytical ability. The worst quality is petty criticism. A key phrase is "I analyze." Virgo's personality is nothing if not practical. You can be attentive to details to the point of obsession. Virgo has an encyclopedic memory for detail, and can often recall casual references to minor subjects. You thrive on meticulous examination of the facts, and are able to manipulate statistics easily.

You can organize the thoughts and ideas of others into a working whole. Your orderly approach to most subjects ensures that you will not overlook any significant information in your pursuit of an answer. Once you have completed an analysis, you can seem to be arbitrary in your decisions. Never think, though, that you have not considered the question first. Virgo can be ingenious at dissecting a problem to get to the heart of a matter.

You are worldly. You understand the nature of material reality. You are fastidious about your own appearance, and often have an orderly home, office, and vehicle. Virgo is a good follower, but as you progress through life you accumulate the knowledge and experience to make you a good leader. Your analytical style does not have the flamboyant energy of Leo, unless you have planets in Leo, but your dependability and honesty are strong management traits. Virgo tends to judge by results.

Virgo's disposition is discerning and critical. You are able to discriminate among diverse offerings and identify the best and worst qualities in people or things. You inquire into the why and how of things as much as into the concrete facts of what, where, and when. As a rule, you are economical in decision-making. You tend to buy quality and conserve your possessions. The intestines and sympathetic nervous system fall under Virgo's rulership. Gray and navy blue are good colors for Virgo.

Libra

⎯⎯ The best quality of Libra lies in your natural social skills. The worst quality is your capacity to vacillate. A key phrase is "I balance."

The Libran personality is, as a rule, peaceful, although you can be a formidable champion of justice when aroused. You are changeable, willing to go along with the decisions of others in all cases where the outcome is not of deep personal importance to you. The tendency to be indecisive may change as you gather experience, but you may always go through a "what if" scenario or two before choosing a course of action.

Vacillation has its positive side—adaptability. Libra is willing to dabble in many different areas, and this is how you gather enough information to hold your own in any social situation. You can be a perfectionist in matters of personal importance, and can surprise others with occasional definitive expressions of your ideas and ideals.

The Libran temperament is sensitive and refined. There is an artistic quality to your mental and emotional outlook—you seek harmony in all things. Libra goes along with the group, but this does not mean you are submissive. You are fully able to hold your own ground intellectually. You often supply the argument that leads to synthesis and equilibrium.

The Libran disposition is sympathetic and kind. You are considerate, and would never think of intentionally causing harm. You enjoy social interaction and can meet others with impartiality. You are often approving of the actions of others. In leadership positions, you will find gentle ways to point out the proper path.

The desire to be around other people inspires a cooperative attitude. Your clarity of communication can make Librans an inspiration to others—when you express your beliefs, you reveal your ideals, your creative sense, and your ability to integrate data into a balanced assessment of the needs of the moment. You appreciate the efforts of others. The parts of the body ruled by Libra are the kidneys and lumbar region. Indigo blue is Libra's color.

Scorpio

♏ The best quality of Scorpio is resourcefulness. The worst quality is the ability to cause trouble. A key phrase is "I desire."

Intensity is the principal personality trait of Scorpio. Whatever career or avocational interests you pursue, you do it with tremendous force. The strength of desire is seen in every serious effort a Scorpio makes. You are proud, and can become the nemesis of anyone who insults you.

Scorpio's mental process is meditative. You can take a set of data and ponder it, penetrating the surface evidence to find deeper meaning. You can cope with difficult and disagreeable tasks because you understand that such tasks will eventually be completed, and you will return to the center of life's current none the worse for the effort, and perhaps stronger for the experience of surviving under pressure.

Secretive and intense, Scorpio's temperament is sometimes difficult to tolerate. These very qualities, however, are part of the magnetism that draws people to you.

The intensity can be expressed through healing or destructive energy, and only you can determine which way you will go. Probably no sign indicates a stronger will. Personal experience teaches Scorpio how to direct that will.

Scorpio often is rather reserved. You are unyielding to the sorts of pressure that work well with other signs, and often do well in careers where independent action is encouraged. Your ability to focus on a single task and put all your energy into it is often seen as skillful. You are often respected for your determination, but perhaps not loved, due to the fact that you are not a manipulator of gentle energies.

No one can exert the pressure that Scorpio can. You make devoted friends who will tell the truth boldly. When you lie, the lies are equally bold, and it may not be possible to tell the difference. The trained Scorpio mind seldom has to resort to a lie, as the truth is seen as a much stronger weapon. Desire lies at the root of all Scorpian action. Scorpio's color is crimson. The parts of the body ruled by Scorpio are the genitals.

Sagittarius

↗ The best quality of Sagittarius is loyalty. This is true for Sun sign Sagittarians, and also for people with other planets in this sign, although with other planets, loyalty may extend only to matters concerning that planet. The worst quality is indiscriminate game-playing. A key phrase is "I aspire."

Sagittarius' personality is generous, ambitious, and loyal. Self-reliant, you can go off on world travels alone without a qualm, and tend to throw yourself into life with the same energy you would pack for such a trip. Your ability to make effective decisions can be an asset in executive positions. You reveal your enthusiasm and positive attitude toward life.

You like to travel mentally, as well. You can study subjects deeply, and enjoy philosophical conversations. You tend to be somewhat conservative, as you would expect for your time of year—it is the conservative harvesting of summer's bounty that feeds us in December, after all. Once you understand the theory of a subject, you are able to take effective action in the practical realm.

Chapter Five

The Sagittarian temperament is outspoken and frank. In fact, sometimes you may wish you could restrain your speech. Still, you are usually open-minded, able to listen to what others have to say. You tend to hold to your own opinions tenaciously, yet you are able to change your mind when a suitable argument is presented. Generally able to make quick decisions, you can be too hasty at times.

Sagittarius is usually proper in demeanor. You can give or take orders, are a solid companion, and are able to share leadership cheerfully. When you engage in sports, you learn the rules and abide by them, just as you respect the rules in all areas of life. Your understanding can come across as magnanimous at times, and at other times you seem self-righteous. You aspire to lofty heights and may be disappointed if others do not attain the same level. You seek to comprehend, both on an interior basis and on a practical level. Once you understand the dynamics of a situation, you cheerfully accept your proper role. Sagittarius' color is light blue. Sagittarius rules the hips and thighs.

Capricorn

♑ The best quality of Capricorn is diplomacy. The worst quality is deceitfulness. A key phrase is "I utilize."

To understand Capricorn, one must understand that there is not much difference between diplomacy and deceit. You tend to be honest and conscientious in your dealings with other people, but you may learn through experience to not say everything you know. You have the capacity to take the practical path to a material goal and leave the precise truth to someone else. That said, Capricorn is a responsible, self-disciplined sign. You can be very patient in the pursuit of your goals, and you generally act on a well-defined sense of moral right and wrong. You recognize and accept duty as a part of life.

Thoughtful and methodical, Capricorn is the master of synthesis. You are methodical and organized in your thinking. Persistence is a quality that you cultivate. You find power in self-control and mental concentration.

By temperament you are cautious. You are subtle about how you gather information and about how you apply your efforts to any task. You make a good manager because of your excellent sense of organization, but you can brood or be overly exacting in your expectations. You can adapt situations to your own needs. You tend to be somewhat conventional in dress and demeanor.

Capricorn is able to take advantage of circumstances. You are mentally prepared to take action when the time is right, and you are efficient in your actions. You can appear unsympathetic to the needs of others, yet you faithfully fulfill what you see as your duty. While you sometimes seem rigid or selfish in your behavior, you are capable of self-sacrifice and are not unjust in your actions. Going back to the key phrase, "I utilize," it is helpful to remember that you make skillful use of the people and situations around you, and you are generally not concerned about the popularity of your actions. The knees and lower legs are ruled by Capricorn. Good colors for Capricorns are black and green.

Aquarius

The best quality of Aquarius is a humanitarian attitude. The worst quality is argumentativeness. A key phrase is "I know."

You are seen as progressive. When we speak of the Age of Aquarius, we are speaking of a period beginning now and extending into the future, with all the possibilities that the future has to offer. As an Aquarian, you may be well-informed or even visionary in your thinking. You may not be grounded in the practical application of your ideas. Focused on a universal goal, you may not attend to the needs of individuals in ordinary circumstances.

You have advanced ideas. You are original and scientific in your methods, and are strongly interested in education, for yourself and for others. You often prefer to learn through conversation with others, rather than strictly through book studies. There is an unconventional quality in your thinking—you can take apples and oranges and make something greater of them.

The Aquarian is generally pleasant, but also is assertive. Your determination can turn to argument when you don't get your way. Your temperament is affected by the external world. You can become cranky or even rebellious at times. Your usually cheerful manner and understanding of human nature make you a skillful social being, but you may be somewhat reclusive, because you need a lot of private time to think things through. You are not terribly practical and have to learn to manage time and money.

An Aquarian is generally kind and is influenced by the kindness of others. This may be because you have moments when you are unsympathetic, and you recognize the need for this quality. Because you value your freedom, you respect the freedom of others. You are interested in metaphysical subjects. Your lack of demonstrative behavior may be your way of keeping your feelings to yourself. Aquarius' color is bright blue. The parts of the body ruled by Aquarius are the ankles.

Pisces

The best quality of Pisces is sympathy. The worst quality is hypersensitivity. A key phrase is "I believe." The Piscean personality is dreamy and idealistic. You like to float in an ocean of sensitivity, relating to your own feelings and the feelings of others directly. You are the classic romantic who wants to indulge the senses. You sometimes appear to be vague.

Mentally, a Piscean is prudent, and balances emotions with a capacity to worry about details. Because your strength lies in the feeling realm, you may feel inferior in the mental realm. It is important to remember that the capacity for sound judgment lies as much in feelings as in logic. Pisces uses psychic senses to make decisions, and may need to learn how to back up these impressions with facts.

Pisces mirrors the environment. Your appearance can change dramatically in different situations. You can be responsive to the needs of others. More than that, you can inspire other people through your own emotional strength. You may be able to see into the future, but this very ability takes you out of the present, and, therefore, may keep you from completing projects.

Pisces is a peaceful sign. You often are retiring, preferring to be a bystander rather than in the middle of the action. You tend to worry and may feel slighted by others. You believe what you feel.

The great strength of Pisces lies in the ability to respond in two worlds—the world of practical social dealings and the internal world of mystical experience. You may need to develop the strengths of planets in other signs to get you around in the day-to-day world, but you are well-equipped to understand the realm of spirit. Your adaptability usually gets you what you need on the material side, even while you have your minds on utopian quests. Compassion can be one of your strongest qualities. Pisces rules the feet. Pisces' color is sea green.

Chapter Six

The Planets, Ascendant, and Midheaven

The planets (including the Sun and Moon) are the actors in the astrological drama. They represent ten general categories of energy—ten subpersonalities—that reflect facets of your personality and ways that you function in the world. Each planet has its own character that is similar to the mythological character after which it was named. You may want to investigate the myths surrounding your favorite planet!

In addition to the Sun, Moon, and eight planets other than Earth, most astrologers consider other points in the chart:

- the Ascendant (or rising sign), and

- the Midheaven.

There are some other considerations in a personal reading. These are not as commonly used, and depend on in-depth study that not all astrologers undertake. These astrological features are not discussed here, but you can expect to find reference to these features in some astrological readings:

- the nodes of the Moon,
- Chiron and asteroids,
- Midpoints between planets, and
- Arabic parts.

This chapter describes each of the planets, the Ascendant, and the Midheaven. In the book we have included the symbols that you see in your chart with their description.

The Sun

The Sun rules Leo. Vitality is the energy reflected by the Sun in the astrological chart. Just as the Sun is the source of life for all living things we know of, the Sun's position in your chart is an indicator of the way you approach life.

Nearly everyone knows their Sun sign and a little bit about it. We read the astrology column in the newspaper to see how the day will be for our sign. Many people like the time of year around their birthday, not just because it is near their birthday, but because the energy of the Sun sign is so comfortable.

Young children express the Sun sign energy clearly and directly. We tend to move away from this clarity as we learn different forms of expression, yet we always come back to the foundation of the Sun sign, learning to perfect the strengths that it indicates and to compensate for any weaknesses. The Sun is, in addition to being the source of life, the sustainer of our individual character. When you understand the deeper nature of your Sun sign, you also understand the core direction for your personal expression in the world.

The house position of the Sun in your chart indicates one area of life that takes on greater importance than any other. It is the area where you are perhaps the most self-conscious, it is where your will can be best expressed, and it is where you can develop the greatest arrogance. You will focus loyalty and generosity in that area, as well as discover your own personal dignity.

The house and sign of the Sun indicates an area in which you will strive to express yourself, and you will want to be recognized for your activities in that area of life. As you gain experience in living, you may become bolder in your efforts to attain your Sun sign goals. You can become a leader in this area because you understand the deepest and broadest values of this area of your life.

When you read about your Sun sign, take the details to heart. Make a personal effort—use your will—to develop the highest and best expression of this sign. It is your birthright, and the area where you can learn to speak and act with authority.

The Moon

The Moon is in its sign of rulership in Cancer. The Moon is visible to us because of reflected light from the Sun. Its monthly motion through the heavens and its phases are timers we should all take seriously. Hospital employees tell stories of increased birth rates or emergency room traffic as the Full Moon approaches. Astrologers know that important activities are best begun just after the New Moon.

The Moon in your chart reflects your subconscious mind. Its sign and house describe your emotional bias—the way you express your feelings most easily and directly.

It is interesting to note that the Sun and Moon appear to be exactly the same size in the sky. If this were not so, we could not have total eclipses of the Sun. But what does this mean to the astrologer? It means that the vitality of the Sun is equal in importance to the action of the Moon in your life. The expression of your individuality is equal in importance to the nurturance of your emotional well-being. Conscious awareness is equal to subconscious motivations. Studying your Moon sign can provide clue to your inner life and suggest paths to increased personal satisfaction with life.

In terms of career, the Sun may show what you want to be when you grow up, but the Moon shows the path—the means—to that end. (This relationship happens to be true for all kinds of astrological charts—for events, nations, weather forecasting, etc.) Learning about the sign and house of your Moon will provide answers to many questions you may have about how to take positive action. This is the area of the chart that shows your emotional changeability, and it also reflects your best path to any other kind of change in your life.

Finally, the Moon shows, by its sign and house, how and where you can be comfortable. It suggests the physical surroundings, the material objects, and the emotional tone that is pleasant for you. It also shows how you assimilate—food, information, or emotional vibrations.

The Sun and Moon together form a team. You will find that be considering them together, you get a fuller, richer sense of who you are and how you can become happier and more successful.

Mercury

☿ Mercury is in its rulership in two signs:
Gemini and Virgo. Mercury was the
messenger of the gods, and the planet is the
fastest in motion. It moves back and forth
through the sky, changing its apparent
direction six times each year. This apparent
back and forth movement is a reflection of
how we learn. We listen, then we try. We go
back to correct a pattern and we try again.
Once we grasp a concept we can move forward quickly to the next challenge.

Our mental processes have two basic
patterns. Inductive reasoning is something
we are born with. It is the capacity to
remember an experience and apply it to
future situations. "Once burned, twice shy"
is one way of looking at inductive reasoning. The other is deductive reasoning. This
is the ability to take a number of observa-
tions and draw conclusions from the information. This is the ability of abstract
thought. Statistical research has inductive
qualities. If we ask ten people if they like a
certain candy and six say yes, we tend to
assume that approximately sixty out of a

hundred will like it too. Sherlock Holmes used deductive reasoning, putting several seemingly unrelated facts together to learn about his quarry.

Mercury provides us with a specific path for both kinds of reasoning, based on its sign and house placement. Mercury, more than any other planet, takes on the attributes of its sign, house, and aspects. Just as the god Mercury delivered a message without changing it, Mercury in your chart shows how you deliver your personal message. The sign shows your personal bias—how you typically choose to express yourself—and the house shows the area of life in which self-expression is the most important to you.

Mercury in your chart shows the speed and quality of communication. It indicates how you use the senses. It shows the area of your life where the reasoning processes can best be exercised. Thus it shows where you are likely to achieve the clearest and most potent expression of your inner thoughts to others. Aspects from other planets show how your communication is influenced by the events and people around you.

Venus

♀ Venus is the goddess of beauty, and is the ruler of Taurus and Libra. She makes everyone feel comfortable. She has a positive outlook on life and imparts that feeling to others. Venus in your chart may indicate, by its sign and house, the part of your body that is most attractive, or a part of the body that you find attractive in others. The seductive part of your personality can be described by looking at Venus. This capacity is clearly not restricted to sexuality, but extends into every area of your life. Venus shows how you can convince others, not through force of will, but through a magnetic attraction.

As an indicator of how you interact well with others, Venus does not suggest co-dependence. It does suggest interdependence, something that has been essential for human development. Babies have a perfection of form that makes us fall in love with them. Movie stars are dressed and made up to be as attractive as possible. Politicians demonstrate the magnetic charisma that convinces us to vote for them, sometimes in spite of all logic.

There is a rhythm to this magnetic attraction and beauty. We get closer to someone to find out what they are like, and then we withdraw to consider how we are feeling about what we discovered. The sign and house Venus occupy describe how all of these functions work. It shows what we like, what about us is the most attractive, and how we engage in the interactivity of human life. It shows how we approach companionship in general.

Venus also indicates where we look for harmony in our lives. When you seek cooperation from others, you want it to fit in with your ideal of harmony. Thus, whatever the context, you will put your personal spin on the situation, molding other people to suit your thoughts on how things work best. Occasionally you may find that the way you want to do things is not practical in the situation, or doesn't work so well for other people. By understanding Venus in your chart, you can develop alternative methods that both achieve the desired goal and provide a level of comfort for you personally. This refinement process is indicted by Venus' sign, house, and aspects.

Mars

♂ Mars rules Aries. Mars is energy. It is the kind of energy that your body uses to contract muscles, to assimilate food, and to fire synapses in the brain. It is the kind of energy that makes gasoline burn, that pushes pistons up and down, and that propels your car. It is the dynamic energy of all action in the material world.

The god Mars was responsible for two distinctive kinds of energetic activity: He was the god of war, sowing terror and fear in the enemy and inspiring courage, but he was also a god of agriculture, who encouraged the planting and tending of crops.

The sign and house of Mars show where your personal energies tend to go when you do not guide them. It also shows where you can concentrate your energy through decisive action for the strongest results. There is a certain reckless quality to Mars. This planet is associated with sharp instruments and vigorous force. We need to understand this planet in order to manage energy well, or it can become angry and destructive. Reading about Mars in your chart can provide answers to your questions about why some situations may have turned out badly, and how to use your physical and emotional energy more successfully in the future.

Mars is also the planet of desire. We all tend to use our energy to get what we want when we want it. Desire is a good thing, because it impels us forward to something new and better. It helps us to find partners and mates. It helps us to find food, clothing, and shelter. On the mental level, desire helps us to choose an area of study, or to select books or movies we want to experience. On a still higher level, Mars indicates the direction of our spiritual passion. It shows what religious or spiritual path will satisfy our desire to understand the universe and master our own actions.

The aspects of Mars in your chart indicate the directions in which you can most easily direct your physical, mental, emotional, and spiritual energies. Understanding Mars helps you to direct your actions to gain the best results.

Jupiter

♃ Jupiter is in its rulership in Sagittarius. Jupiter is the planet that can tell you about processes in your life. On the physical level Jupiter relates to glandular function, specifically the liver. The sign and house placement indicate the general level of glandular function, and may indicate the most appropriate diet. Aspects to Jupiter can indicate the timing of diet and nutritional changes to achieve healthier processing within the body.

The same is true for the mind. Jupiter indicates a philosophical level of thinking. Its placement and aspects suggest how you relate to the world on the mental level, where you thoughts tend to expand, and how you approach new situations mentally. Jupiter reflects the area where you are most optimistic about life. It can also show where you can become extravagant or how you tend to exaggerate.

Jupiter also shows how you approach religious concepts. Do you examine the details like Virgo? Do you go with what is comfortable in Taurean style? Jupiter shows how you come to understand the Universe and God, what inspires you to greater faith, and how you hold on to your beliefs once they have developed.

Jupiter is idealistic. Its placement and aspects show where idealism will take you during your life. Jupiter provides a reflection of how you pursue your mission in life. Here I am referring to your spiritual mission, but also to your career as that pertains to your spiritual development.

Jupiter reflects the human capacity for forgiveness. Each of us has a personal style where relationships are concerned, and each of us forgives the errors and differences in others. Jupiter's placement and aspects show how we learn to forgive ourselves for weaknesses and mistakes. This is how we come to understand ourselves, not as vessels of perfect human expression, but rather as spiritually guided beings who seek our own most inspired, most confident, most successful expression. Jupiter allows us to indulge in excesses, while at the same time guiding us to our goals. This planet shows how your individual sense of humor works. Through Jupiter we come to

understand humanity in general and ourselves in particular, both aspiring to be
spiritually wise and understanding of self
and others.

Saturn

♄ Where Jupiter showed process, Saturn
shows structure. Saturn is the ruler of
Capricorn. Its placement and aspects indicate how structure is perceived either as
limitation and restriction that keep you
from pursuing your desires or as a container in which you can lead an orderly and
productive life. On the whole, structure is a
good thing. The structure of bones allows
us to move about and stand erect. Our skin
provides a container without which we
would surely die. It is how we perceive the
container and what we do with it that
makes all the difference.

As Saturn moves through the signs, its
cycle defines major life changes. Around age
seven you develop a new sense of personal
responsibility, and at about fifteen you
become a young adult, able to use abstract
thinking in your decision-making process.

At age twenty-one you become an adult in the eyes of the law, and at around ages twenty-eight to thirty you experience your first Saturn Return (it takes Saturn twenty-eight to thirty years to go through all of the signs one time), and you undergo a shift from an extended growth period into an extended productive period. This structure is more or less the same for everyone.

The sign and house placement of Saturn indicate how you can best pursue your career, whatever that career may be. Should you start out owning your own company in Leo's style, or should you undertake humanitarian goals, like an Aquarian? By following Saturn's indicators you can plan a career course that allows a steady development. (Llewellyn offers "Opportunities," an astrological service that tells you about your career potential and that can help you to choose your first, second, or even third career based on astrology. See page 178 for information on how to get an astrological interpretation of your career potential.)

Saturn provides a barometer for you in the form of feedback. Sometimes you feel limited in what you can do, and you can use this as feedback about what educational opportunity to pursue. Sometimes you are afraid of the next step, and you can use this fear to show you where to seek emotional support. You will experience authority and responsibility in your life in constructive or destructive ways, based on where Saturn is found. Saturn can become your inner teacher and guide, as well as a timer for major changes throughout your life.

Uranus

Uranus rules Aquarius. If you have wondered why and how sudden changes come into your life, look no further. Uranus may be the answer. This planet reflects the energy of sudden change and also provides the intuitive information you need to deal with beginnings, endings, and even catastrophes.

Let's look at the independent, unconventional actions inspired within us and reflected by Uranus in the chart. This planet shows what part of your life will be the focus of your independence and where you will take an unconventional approach to family, career, or relationships—everything. Disruptive ideas and events come along to bring you back into balance. Have you noticed that the more eccentric your behavior, the more life gives you a push and forces you to conform? This is Uranian energy working to bring you back into balance.

Next consider the role of intuition in your daily life. As you have disruptive episodes, you begin to be able to anticipate them, making adjustments ahead of time to minimize the upset. For example, once you slide on the ice a few times you learn how to keep your balance. Then you learn how to control a skid while driving a car. Then you understand how to manage a spiritual disruption more easily. This is due to your developing intuition—you can foresee the future partly because of past experiences themselves and partly because you recall intuitive flashes that preceded or accompanied them. Uranus shows how this works for you personally.

When you find yourself detaching from people and events, this is Uranus in action.

You have the capacity to take an aloof position—a more analytical and less active role in situations. The placement and aspects of Uranus show how you can best achieve an impersonal attitude in the face of difficulty (or it shows you how to remain connected in those moments when you would really rather be doing something else). This energy focuses your attention on invisible, inner perceptions of your world in a way that is similar to everyone in your age group (your generation has Uranus in the same zodiac sign), yet utterly personal in its development and expression, based on the house placement and aspects to other planets.

Neptune

♆ Neptune is in its rulership in Pisces. All that is glamorous, mystical, metaphysical, and inspirational participates in the energy reflected by Neptune in your chart. Like Uranus, Neptune and Pluto remain in one sign for many years, so your generation shares a similar grasp of Neptune's energy. The house placement and the aspects to Neptune color your sensitivity in a more personal way.

What you consume is what you are on the physical plane. The placement of Neptune indicates how you assimilate food, drink, medications, and other drugs. It shows your tolerance for foods and other substances, and indicates where your physical system can get out of balance most easily. Neptune indicates an area where care can prevent or lessen harm.

Confusion and deception are part of the Neptune's picture. Vagueness and glamour can be part of fraudulent activity, or they can be the essence of entertainment. Magic shows are all about deceiving our senses in order to surprise and entertain us. Neptune's placement shows your level of susceptibility to deceit and your level of ability as well.

Imagination is part of Neptune's realm. Your creative style depends on the ability to use your feelings and intellect to make something new and different. Problem-solving means imagining solutions and then trying them on for size mentally before rushing into action. Dreams are a function of this energy, and Neptune's placement can show a lot about the nature of your dreams and their role in your life.

Spirituality is a significant part of human life. Neptune speaks to this area by showing you what area of your life needs a spiritual boost. It also show you what career or other activity will satisfy your inner spiritual yearning. Neptune's movement through your chart will indicate times when spiritual measures are called for.

Psychic impressionability is in Neptune's realm. Your ability to tune in to others can be defined by examining Neptune in your chart. Your best path to psychic development may be described by Neptune's placement and aspects.

Pluto

Pluto is represented by two glyphs: ♇ stands for Percival Lowell, who discovered Pluto, while ♇ is commonly used by astrologers. Pluto is the god of the Underworld. His actions are mysterious and even frightening. The planet was discovered in the 1930s at a time when the underworld of gangsters was thriving, causing serious disruption and turmoil. The power of such activities is only one expression of Pluto's energy. Pluto is the ruler of Scorpio.

Obsessive thinking and compulsive action are indicated by Pluto. The house position and aspects of Pluto show where you can get caught up in destructive thought patterns and activities that are not in your best interest or do not serve the general welfare of people. Often the impulse behind such activities is control at any cost, regardless of the results.

Transitions and transformations of all kinds are a broader expression of Plutonian urges. The god of the Underworld rules over death. Pluto in your chart can indicate how you face and accept major changes in your life and in the lives of family and friends. It shows the kind of events that come into your life due to outside forces, and, therefore, how you develop flexible responses to pressure.

All invisible activities are part of the Plutonian picture. You may find that many people in your age group share your views concerning ESP, psychic forces, and things

magical. You also will find that you see particular uses for such energy, and your use
will be different from theirs. You may feel
this is of greater or lesser importance in
your life. Learning about Pluto's place in
your chart can set you on a path of discov-
ery of your own "magic."

Transmutation and rejuvenation are not
the least important of Pluto's expressions.
By learning to control less constructive
impulses and actions, you can channel
your energy into positive directions like
hands-on or spiritual healing, strengthening your body's immune system, and generally revitalizing every area of experience.
As you come to understand your hidden
urges and control your responses to outside influences, you can experience a rich
diverse experience on all levels—you will
have choice.

The Ascendant

The Ascendant or rising sign reflects your
persona—what you choose to show to the
world. Whereas the Sun sign is your individuality and does not change a great deal,

you have the capacity to choose the nature and level of expression of your Ascendant. You can choose the most destructive expression, or you may choose to show a side of yourself to the world that is full of optimism and promise.

The Ascendant is frequently useful in describing your physical characteristics and general health. Aside from geographical and ethnic realities, the rising sign shows complexion, hair and eye color, stature, and weight. A Gemini would be rather taller than average, and Taurus might be on the stocky side, within the range of genetic tendencies.

The Ascendant offers suggestions for what kind of clothing looks good, and what colors will make you seem stronger. The general shape of the head and face are linked to the Ascendant. The sign also indicates a part of the body that you can show off to good advantage. It may not be your favorite part of yourself, but it is one that will respond to careful treatment in terms of clothing, movement, etc. The Taurus may not think about the throat very much, but this is a key area to focus on to create a strong effect on others. Aquarians can benefit from careful selection of shoes, as the ankles are "the thing."

As you learn about your Ascendant, you will find a whole array of new considerations for how to present yourself to the world. Should you be flippant or stern, gregarious or darkly serious? The rising sign can provide a wealth of imaginative possibilities.

Because the Ascendant is the way others see you, physically and in every other way, it pays to understand what they are seeing. You can develop a whole range of clothing, movements, communication styles, and general attitudes based on your rising sign. You can overcome limitations in other areas by emphasizing the positives here. In this way you actively participate in creating the impression you want others to have, and you become more influential as you project a well thought-out image.

Chapter Six

The Midheaven

As mentioned in the introductory material, the Midheaven is the first point in the chart to be calculated. The Midheaven is the part of the zodiac that is the highest (most elevated), visible point in the sky at the time you are born. If you ask the question, "How long has it been since zero degrees of Aries was at the Midheaven?" the answer tells you what degree of the zodiac is there in terms of time. If the Sun is at zero degrees of Aries, the Sun will be at the Midheaven at noon. Noon in this case is based on local time. Standard and daylight time can affect the Sun's position, placing it to one side or the other of the Midheaven point.

The Midheaven reflects what you know—or can know—about yourself. It represents ego-consciousness. Infants have little or no boundary between Self and Other. As children grow and learn, they come to understand themselves as separate beings, and they learn to depend on their own intelligence, emotions, and skills. In short, they learn about themselves as they learn about the world. The Midheaven reflects this self-awareness.

Psychologically healthy adults have a clear sense of Self, distinguished from Other. They know what their core motivations are, and they know what skills they have to achieve their physical, mental, emotional, and spiritual goals. The sign the Midheaven occupies indicates the nature of self-understanding, and provides the springboard from which you can dive into the process of gaining ego consciousness—understanding of what moves you on a deep personal level.

The Midheaven offers a way to understand yourself better, and is key to developing a flexible ego. We all know people who seem brittle and inflexible. We sense that they might "break" if they are pushed too hard in certain areas. Flexibility means developing an ego structure that can withstand the onslaught of life experiences and adapt or adjust to them. Astrology points out one path toward the development of broad-based, ego skills, and it describes both the limitations of your ego and the positive potential of self-awareness.

Chapter Seven

The Houses

Your chart is divided into twelve sections called houses. They are numbered from the left side counterclockwise around the chart. The chart represents the planets against a background of the signs of the zodiac, and these signs rise in clockwise motion. Thus the First House (number one) rises first, and so on. Each house includes part of one or more signs. Depending on where you were born, and the time of day, one house may include two or three signs. The farther you were born from the equator, the more likely this is to happen. There are different ways to calculate the houses, based on time or distance. Some astrologers prefer a system in which all the houses are an even thirty degrees, just like the signs of the zodiac. One method that has been proven to work with timing of events is the Koch System, named after its developer. That is the system used in the charts in this book.

Each of the houses represents an area of your life. The planets tell you what energy is involved and the signs indicate how that energy will express itself. The houses tell you where in your life the effect will be felt. The houses follow a logical order that parallels the signs to some extent. They move from the personality (First House) toward significant others (Seventh House), and from the home (Fourth House) to public life (Tenth House). All areas of experience can be found in one of the houses.

The First House

The First House begins at the Ascendant at the left side of the chart. It lies below the horizon line. The Ascendant is one of the strongest points in the chart. It is the point that was rising in the east at your birth time and place. (The Ascendant is discussed in chapter 6.)

The First House focuses on what you show to the world. This includes the physical body and its appearance. It also includes the personality. Both of these are factors over which you have some degree of control. You *can* decide how to dress and how to act. You can choose to show the best of the rising sign. The First House also describes general qualities of appearance that you cannot control. Gemini rising indicates a relatively tall person, while Taurus indicates a relatively stocky build, for example.

The Sun shows your individuality. The Ascendant may sound like it does the same, but the focus is on personality. We all know people who have one kind of personality that we can see, but when we get to know them, we find something different beneath the exterior they show to us. It is that way with the Ascendant. It is the mask we show to others. There are eleven other houses that describe how we are in the world from different points of view.

The First House indicates the constitution and vitality of the physical body. Earth signs suggests a solid, grounded constitution, while air signs indicate a lighter quality that seems to float. Fire signs indicate a fiery temperament and vitality that comes in flashes, while water signs may indicate a constitution that has a rhythmic quality— an ebb and flow of energy.

When planets are in this house they have the fullest capacity for expression. The planet's energy seems to come through a wide open door into your life. This is also true of the Fourth, Seventh, and Tenth Houses. If there is a planet in the First House, its nature is prominent in the personality. If there is no planet here, then you consider the planet that "rules" the sign, and also Mars. These influences will be less forceful than planets in the house.

The Second House

The Second House indicates how you extend your personality into the world. In children this is the two-and-one-half to five-year-old stage of development, when you move outside the family nucleus and begin to make friends in a larger neighborhood. The immediate surroundings often determine the level of self-esteem. If the surroundings are secure and warm, the self prospers, while a lack of security can cause self-doubt and fear to arise.

Possessions and self-esteem are two important components of the immediate physical and emotional environment. It's interesting that these two things are found in the same house in the chart, as we don't consciously associate them with each other. When you think about it, though, it is true that what you have is often a big part of your self-esteem. Much of what we consume is chosen to make us feel better about ourselves.

Your feelings in general are part of the Second House. Beginning with your basic comfort level and reaching into deeper emotions, this house can tell you a lot about your emotional approach to life. Any planets in this house color the nature of the sign on the cusp (the sign at the beginning of the house).

The Second House also has to do with how you actually get money and material things. The sign indicates the method—the kind of effort needed to obtain income. Planets in the Second House indicate the people and activities involved. If you don't have any planets here, don't worry. The plant associated with the Second-House sign(s) will show where the money comes from, based on the house where it is found. For example, if you have Taurus on the Second House cusp and Venus in the Sixth House, then your money comes from the work environment. If Venus were in the Twelfth House, by contrast, then your income comes from private activities. If Mars is in the Second House, then some energetic activity may be involved in creating income.

How you define your personal security is a Second-House issue. The sign and any planets, by their nature, indicate what security means for you personally. You may have noticed that the things that make you happy and secure are different from other family members or your friends. Some people need a nurturing environment (Cancer in the Second House), while others are footloose and need their freedom (Aquarius on the cusp or Uranus in the house) to feel truly secure.

The Third House

Siblings and the immediate neighborhood are what you experienced in childhood between the ages of five and seven and one half. This is the next step out into the world beyond the immediate environment of the Second House. You may have been allowed to go a certain distance from home by yourself when you were this age—across the street to a friend's house, for example.

How you tend to think is determined in early childhood, and thus is represented by the Third House. By the age of seven and one half most of us have clearly defined ego structure—we understand that we are separate and different from other people, and we begin to understand how we are capable of determining the course of our lives. Many lifelong opinions are formed at this early age, based on family and neighborhood environments.

Early education is a Third-House matter. This is another powerful factor in the shaping of thought processes that last a lifetime. Learning begins before you are born, but those first years of school are critical to the development of reading, mathematical, and logical cognitive processes. The early school experience of learning to read, for example, sets the tone for a lifetime of reading.

Communication of all kinds is a Third-House activity. Planets here show the most direct means of expression. The placement of the house ruler shows another path for communication to take. The sign shows what kind of communication you are most comfortable with—air signs might indicate writing, for example, while earth signs indicate a more concrete medium of expression.

Short trips—trips through your neighborhood—are a Third-House matter. Remember that you are the one to decide what "short" means. What is in the neighborhood for one person could be across state lines, while another person's neighborhood extends only to the nearest main street. Many people feel that day trips are in the neighborhood, even if they involve short airplane flights. Some people feel their neighborhood includes entire nations or continents.

The Fourth House

Your home base can be understood by looking at the Fourth House. Home may always be the place where your mother and father live, or it may be the place where you are hanging your hat today. As with other houses, personal tastes and needs determine the meaning of home. If you grew up in one state, that may always be your home state. Most people want to have certain objects or kinds of things in the home environment that make them comfortable. Hence, all Hilton hotels have the same homey quality because they are staffed by similar people and decorated similarly. Generally speaking, the Hilton is not home.

Just as the home is where you develop the foundation of your beliefs, the Fourth House is where you look for those basic ethical and moral basics that govern your life. Fire signs on the Fourth House may indicate beliefs that are lofty, intuitive conceptions of the world, while earth signs indicate more grounded, practical considerations. Planets in the Fourth indicate the parent or other authority figure from whom you acquired your earliest ideals, most often the father.

The sign on the Fourth House cusp (*Imum Coeli* or IC) indicates the deepest well of your being. The spirit that guides you is represented here, and its energy bubbles up from deep in the unconscious to emerge at the Midheaven (cusp of the Tenth House). If the Midheaven is what you know (or can learn) about yourself, the IC is the source from which that knowledge springs.

The Fifth House

The Fifth House is associated with all forms of creativity: creation, recreation, and procreation. All people have a Fifth House. Whether you have planets here or not, you are a creative being with great potential. By examining this house you can learn about how you use your talents to make a lasting impression on the world around you.

Procreation is one way to become immortal. Children carry on our ideals and enrich our lives every day. The act of conception is an expression of creative sexuality. The act of birthing is a dynamic affirmation of the desire to become a parent. The act of parenting is a lifelong process of working with your children for their highest good, thereby fulfilling your own highest creative potential.

The sign here indicates your general attitude toward children, pets, and playmates. Are you a playful Gemini, flitting from one game to the next while forming lasting friendships? Do your pets become surrogate children, demanding your love and attention, à la Virgo? Perhaps you take your creativity seriously, producing lasting monuments à la Capricorn.

You may not see yourself as particularly talented and creative. Remember, creativity can take many forms. The teacher who teaches students to read well is performing a creative act. The factory worker who takes an active interest in performing his job can be very creative in finding better ways to get the job done. The parent who protects a child from harm and guides the daily activities is actively participating in the creation of a happy, successful adult.

Creativity is found in the approach toward life's activities, and the sign and planets in the Fifth House describe the approach that suits you best.

The Sixth House

Service to others and to yourself is seen in the Sixth House. This includes the work you perform and the work environment. A fire sign here does not mean you have to be a fireman, but it does indicate that your work environment should encourage intuitive and creative thought. Water signs here indicate that you would enjoy working near bodies of water. Earth signs suggest that you will be happier working at ground level. Air signs suggest some branch of the communication industry, perhaps writing or publishing. Air signs may enjoy the upper floors of buildings.

Work habits are also part of the Sixth-House picture. Earth signs may indicate a steady approach to work, while fire signs show an intuitive work-nature that goes in spurts. Water signs may need a contemplative or at least relaxed environment in which ideas and feelings can flow freely. Air signs like lots of communication among people to stimulate ideas. Each sign tells how you approach your day-to-day work activities. It would be helpful for managers and supervisors to understand the Sixth House of each employee and to make modifications in the work environment to suit each individual.

Physical health in general can be defined by looking at the Sixth House. The Ascendant and First House describe the physical body and its appearance. The Sixth House indicates where physical problems may require adjustment in the form of exercise, diet, or medical treatment. The planet that rules the Sixth House is a key factor in health considerations, so its nature should be considered carefully. Other planets here can indicate strong or weak parts of the body.

Your attitude toward your employees and other service providers can be seen in the Sixth House. While you have one approach to dealing with people, they have multiple responses. Learn about the sign on the Sixth House so that you can bring more flexibility into your dealings with employees, and you will find they respond more freely to your requests. You can be aware of individual styles without sacrificing your own priorities because each sign and planet has the capacity to respond to the others in unique ways.

The Seventh House

The Seventh House tells you about how you relate to significant others, including marriage and business partners. Because marriage is a kind of business, and you may sometimes feel married to your business partner, studying the Seventh House can give you helpful hints about how you choose both, and how you deal with them afterward. Others are significant in our lives and affect the way we feel about ourselves. You may be surprised that you actually look for the same traits in business and romantic partners!

Enemies—open enemies, that is—are seen in the Seventh House. This house is opposite the First House—you and your personality. Open enemies are out there in front of you, making themselves apparent. You may feel you have no actual enemies, but you may be able to relate to the characteristics of people who seem to irritate you for no apparent reason—people who don't seem to have your best interests at heart.

Competitors are not precisely enemies, but they meet the criteria by wanting to be better, do better, or sell more than you. Competition is one way we all grow—we see someone with greater skill and we emulate them, not just for the sake of self-improvement, but also to beat them at their own game. The Seventh House shows some of the key qualities of your competitor.

Your attitude toward partnership is seen in the Seventh House. If you have no planets here, you can still have a marriage or business partnership. It may not be the most important thing in your life, or you may find that the person you marry came to you through the activities of another house—where the ruler of the Seventh House is found. If you have the Sun in the Seventh, partners may be one of the most important things in your life. Planets here show how you tend to deal with significant others of all kinds. The sign shows qualities you look for in others.

The sign in the Seventh House often is attractive to you because you project your unconscious desires there. These individuals may have both the best and the worst traits you desire in a mate—they are able to speak to your subconscious in ways you are unaware of.

The Eighth House

The Eighth House covers sex, death, and other people's resources. Most beginning astrologers question how these areas of life are related, and the explanation offers insight into some of life's most intriguing activities. The lives of others impact our lives on a moment-to-moment basis. Every human interaction engages the mental, emotional, material, or spiritual resources of at least one other person. Sexual response and sexual expression form a fundamental area for us to cultivate the spiritual connection with others through the physical connection. Death focuses on the separation from another person who has been significant in our lives, and at the same time may put us directly in touch with that person's resources in the form of inheritance.

The sign in the Eighth indicates how you express yourself sexually, and how you respond to your partner. Consider the meaning of the sign on the Eighth in the light of intimate behavior and you may be surprised at how accurately that sign describes your sexual desires and needs. Knowing this, you can use the information to satisfy your desires more directly, asking for just the thing you want without having to guess what it is yourself.

What you receive from others in the form of inheritance is an Eighth-House matter, as are banking, insurance, and other financial issues. The sign and planets here indicate how you relate to money and financial matters in general. The aspects to planets in the Eighth show what tendencies and skills you have where money is concerned. If you have no planets here, look for the planet associated with the sign in the Eighth and check out the aspects it makes to see what other areas of your life most directly influence money matters.

Just as the Seventh House relates others to you (First House), the Eighth House connects other people's self-esteem to yours (Second House). Often the evidence of self-worth we see in the behavior of others affects our estimation of ourselves. Your attitude toward birth, death, and self-sacrifice are all part of the way you relate to other people and their values. The Eighth House is a rich source of information about areas of life that we tend to examine only when we are forced to by circumstances and other people.

The Ninth House

The Ninth House governs areas of life that are larger than any one person's perspective. Jupiter, the largest of the planets, is associated with the Ninth House, so the subjects of philosophy, religion, law, and higher consciousness take on the scope of this giant planet.

Higher education and personal studies are Ninth-House matters. Here are found the subjects of college and postgraduate study, as well as lifetime intellectual pursuits. The Ph.D. degree is titled the *doctorate of philosophy* in the subject being studied because the work goes well beyond the art or science of the subject, and delves into its larger, often spiritual, meaning.

Higher consciousness is a natural outgrowth of such studies. First we learn the nuts and bolts of the language of the subject, then we learn the theoretical and practical applications of that information. Only after apprenticeship and practice of the art or craft do we reach the philosophical understanding of the material. Then we may be able to connect to a higher consciousness of the subject and gain a more global or transpersonal understanding.

Long-distance travel takes us as far from our ordinary daily living as we can go. It puts us in situations where we must engage the philosophical application of all that we have learned. We enter a different culture or subculture and we become both teacher and student in that new place. We "soak up the culture" and we share of ourselves. Travel is one way to experience different philosophies and belief systems (Ninth-House concerns).

Legal matters are revealed by the Ninth House. The law is the philosophical framework on which we base social interaction. Laws are a body of agreements for behavior. They have grown out of human experience over millennia. They may require change and adaptation from time to time, but generally they are a reflection of the underlying philosophy of a nation, state, or locality. Many current laws are found in ancient religious texts.

Religious beliefs may not always have the profound depth that study provides, but these beliefs are grounded in the higher, spiritual awareness of the Ninth House. The sign here indicates what the essential quality of religion must deliver to you, whether it be an intellectual system, emotional support structure, or practical set of rules to live by. Religious mystics are in touch with the heart of their relationship to the Universe and God or Goddess.

The Tenth House

Your career is profiled in the Tenth House. The sign and planets here can be used to define one or more broad career paths, and may also provide details about how to choose the focus of career as well. Earth signs indicate careers that deal with material matters. Air signs indicate communication of all kinds. Fire signs may tend toward inspirational and artistic expression, and water signs indicate careers that focus on actual water (like sailing), or metaphorical water (such as careers devoted to change, like psychotherapy and medicine). Most careers include features of all the elements, with a strong focus on one of them, and the sign in the Tenth House is a strong indicator of the basis of your career.

What you know about yourself is indicated by the Tenth House. We have talked about the First House reflecting personality (what you show to the world). The Tenth is what you know or can learn about yourself. The sign here indicates an area where you may be rather touchy, as your ego can become involved here. This is because we use the ego to mediate with the world, and when the world applies pressure, the ego resists to prevent us from being overwhelmed. To the extent that your ego is flexible, you learn about yourself in such encounters, as well as learning about the rest of the world.

Social standing and public image is a Tenth-House matter. This house is at the top of the chart, the most exposed to light. We are exposed in social situations and revealed to the world, sometimes on a ready-or-not basis. When planets move into the Tenth House by transit or progression, you may receive unexpected publicity. What you know about yourself may become public information.

Your attitude toward authority and your way of accepting responsibility are Tenth-House matters. Once you have learned something about yourself, you apply it in your life. The more you learn about the sign in the Tenth House, the better you may understand how responsibility affects you. Then you can accept the authority of your position more easily. This brings us back to career. When you understand how you work with responsibility and authority, you can be more effective in your career.

The Eleventh House

Groups and group activities are Eleventh-House matters. The sign indicates what kind of groups you will be attracted to, and planets here reflect the kinds of people in those groups. Friends are also related to the Eleventh House. Here is where you can learn about the kinds of people who appeal to your deepest being—the people with whom you most want to spend time.

Intellectual pleasure can be thought of as a sort of friend. When you are alone, what do you think and dream about? What subjects interest you? Look to the Eleventh House sign and planets for the answers.

Your attitude toward leadership can be understood by learning about the Eleventh House. Do you take a practical, earth-sign approach to leadership roles? Do you expect leaders to be practical? With a water sign here, do you expect leaders to be understanding, feeling-based individuals, able to read the emotional current of the group? Perhaps you prefer the fiery passionate leader whose charisma carries people into action, or the intellectual, orderly mind whose demands are almost always logical and clear.

Your objectives in life are reflected in the Eleventh House. Just as your personal self-esteem (Second House) follows the First House of your persona, so does your career self-esteem thrive when your goals are achieved (the Eleventh follows the Tenth House of career). This sets up an interesting situation. The signs on these houses are almost always different. Thus, your career may be practical and concrete (earth), but your goals may be more intellectual (air). The process and the goal are strikingly different.

Finally, circumstances beyond your control are reflected in the Eleventh House. We like to think we are on top of life for the most part, but each of us will have to deal with experiences where there is little or nothing that we can do to affect the outcome. How you relate to these events can be understood through the sign and planets here. If an earth sign, then circumstances place you where you cannot affect the material outcome. With a water sign, you may be unable to change the emotional impact of events. Air signs could indicate that logical decisions are made that you must accept. Fire signs could indicate actual fires, or metaphorically inspired events that take you by surprise.

The Twelfth House

Psychic and intuitive processes are the foundation of the Twelfth House. The sign here shows one of the ways in which you engage your intuitive capabilities. Planets indicate the kind of people you invite into your intuitive sphere.

Private matters are in the Twelfth House. The sign shows what you consider to be private and how you manage it. By studying this house, you can learn why other people are secretive about private matters that are of little importance to you, while you choose very differently in this area.

Institutions, such as hospitals, or prisons, are Twelfth-House places. Think of a religious retreat, a convent, or a place where you could spend time alone in contemplation. A hospital is a place where you can go for rest and regeneration, but it is away from your normal daily experience, unless your Twelfth-House interests draw you into a medical profession. Prisons offer a contained environment away from public life for individuals convicted of crimes.

Secret enemies are a Twelfth-House matter. You may not think you have enemies, but most of us know people we do not want to be around, and presumably the feeling can go both ways. The chart of a spy may be filled with the intrigue of secret negotiations, clandestine meetings, and other hidden activities. Most of us will go through life being affected very little by enemies, just as most of us spend rather a small amount of time thinking about harming the people we dislike.

The subconscious level of mind is a sort of secret enemy. We hide matters in the unconscious that we do not want to deal with in our daily lives, and sometimes these unconscious thoughts surface to irritate us, just as an enemy's barb could inflict pain. In the chart, which turns in a clockwise motion, the Twelfth House has just risen over the horizon before your birth. Thus the subconscious contains information about events from the recent or distant past that have a significant effect on your life, whether or not you remember those events. Some astrologers feel that karmic ties can be reflected in the Twelfth House for this reason.

How you "get away" from other people is shown by the sign and planets here. With earth signs you may actually move away. Air signs may cease to communicate, while water signs may freeze up. Fire signs may simply enter an altered state of consciousness where they focus on something different, and are effectively no longer present.

Chapter Eight

The Aspects

How are the planets connected to each other?

The planets relate to each other when they are certain distances apart in the zodiac. These relationships, called aspects, are identified with certain kinds of action. The houses are the area of life in which your drama takes place, the signs are the setting in which action occurs. The planets are the actors, and the aspects show what kind of dialogue and action are most likely to occur.

Even if you don't know your exact birth time, you can consider the aspects (with the exception of those to the Moon), as the planets don't move far enough in one day to change the aspects very much. The Moon moves between eleven and fourteen degrees each day, so its aspects change each hour or so. An exact aspect is one where the planets are the defined number of degrees apart in the sky. Even when they are not exact (and they rarely are), the aspect is still felt. It's a little like a radio station. Even when you are not exactly tuned in, you still receive a signal. But you do have to be close!

What are these lines in the center of my chart?

Each line in the center of the chart links to planets together because they relate to each other in a significant way. Some astrologers believe that every planetary relationship is significant, but most have refined the list to some or all of those in the accompanying chart. I have listed the aspects in order according to what portion of the circle they involve.

Conjunction (360/1 or 0°): Beginnings or endings

Opposition (1/2 or 180°): Awareness of others

Trine (1/3 or 120°): Conditions of ease

Square (1/4 or 90°): Challenges

Quintile (1/5 or 72°) or Biquintile (2/5 or 144°): Talents and creativity

Sextile (1/6 or 60°): Opportunities

Semi-square (1/8 or 45°) or Sesqui-square (3/8 or 135°): Tension or agitation

Semi-sextile (1/12 or 30°): Growth (sometimes through pain)

Quincunx (5/12 or 150°): Adjustment

Conjunction

♂ The conjunction aspect defines the beginning or ending of a circle. It emphasizes the point where two or more planets are, thereby giving them prominence. Therefore, what those planets represent is more prominent than would ordinarily be the case. The energy of the planets is united and magnified. The focus can result in neurotic obsession and its resultant compulsive behaviors. A more normal experience may involve intense action or emotion, but without the negative quality.

Life begins as one cell that houses all the potential for an individual human being. The progressed or transiting conjunction marks the beginning of a new cycle of activity, and the nature of the planets reflects the potential for that activity. Regardless of the nature of the planets, the conjunction itself reminds us of the principal of unity. We reconnect with the fundamental truth represented by each of the planets.

Opposition

The opposition aspect defines a polarity. All sensory awareness is based on polarities. The opposition is the only aspect where a line connecting the two planets will pass through the center of the chart, dividing the chart into equal segments. Many symbols, such as the Tao, are expressions of the polarity of light and dark, left and right. The opposition line also connects the center with the circumference of the chart, symbolizing the connection between inner and outer being.

The awareness created by this polarizing aspect can feel like a separative force. You are connected to something that has been projected by your unconscious in many cases, something you don't wish to acknowledge. The beneficial side of the aspect is that it show you an area where you can learn the value of others or the object outside yourself. The opposition defines substance by defining a polarity between two planets. This establishment of awareness can then lead to the perception of value. Thus the planets in an opposition can be understood to have significance or value as a pair, not just as two different energies.

Robert F. Kennedy has striking oppositions in his birth chart. His awareness of the power of communication and his love of power, the capacity of his emotional arguments to sway his associates, and the sheer energy he applied to his work can be found in these aspects that are all within one degree of exactness.

Trine

△ In childhood development, the perception of self as distinct from the rest of the world is followed by the development of the ego complex, a mediator between Self and Other. The trine aspect connects two planets that are seen to have value relative to each other, but only when they are consciously considered. A trine aspect will do nothing if you make no effort to acknowledge and activate the planetary energies.

The aspect is one of ease—the planets can act together easily and naturally. If the Sun makes a trine, or if two planets form

Robert F. Kennedy
November 20, 1925
Brookline, MA
03:10:00 PM EST
ZONE: +05:00
071W07'00"
42N20'00"

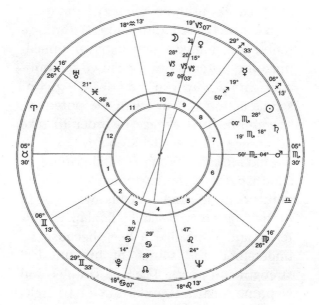

Geocentric
Tropical
Koch Houses

Figure 5. Robert F. Kennedy's Natal Chart.

trines in the same element as the Sun, these aspects will be the easiest to work with consciously. They will just naturally be involved in decision-making processes. The down side of trines is that they may lead to a lazy attitude. You may allow a not so constructive condition to exist and do nothing to change it, or you may not maximize the potential of a positive relationship. Either way, you are not taking conscious action to work with the potential. The mind must engage in order to take advantage of the available energy.

Muhammad Ali's chart contains multiple trine aspects. He understood the grounded nature of his life and used this awareness in his boxing career. He could "float like a butterfly and sting like a bee" because he understood the source of his physical strength and power. The Sun, Uranus, and Neptune form a Grand Trine, or triangle, allowing the energies of these three planets to work very easily together. In earth signs, they gave him patience—he would wait for the right moment in a fight and then suddenly devastate his opponent.

Muhammad Ali
January 17, 1942
Louisville, KY
06:30:00 PM CST
ZONE: +06:00
085W46'00"
38N15'00"

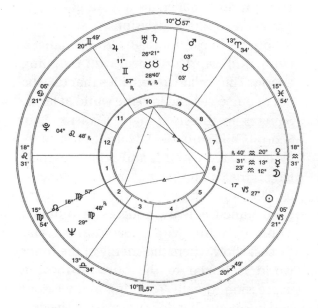

Geocentric
Tropical
Koch Houses

Figure 6. Muhammed Ali's Natal Chart.

131

Square

☐ The square aspect connects you directly to the material world according to the nature of the planets involved. They present challenges to your course of action and demand decisions.

Squares in cardinal signs (Aries, Cancer, Libra, and Capricorn) deal with outgoing energy. They relate to activities that take us out of ourselves and into the world at large. Squares in the fixed signs (Taurus, Leo, Scorpio, and Aquarius) deal with the energy of looking inward, and relate to challenges that we find in our interior processes. The outer appearance of such a square is sustained activity. Squares in mutable signs (Gemini, Virgo, Sagittarius, and Pisces) show where the energy of the inner world is linked to the outward-moving expression directly, resulting in a wisdom and harmony that does not exist in the cardinal and fixed squares. This square is a moving, adaptable, flexible energy. It is not as clear as the other squares because it is

Abraham Lincoln
February 12, 1809
Hodgenville, KY
06:30:00 AM GMT
ZONE: +00:00
085W44'00"
37N34'00"

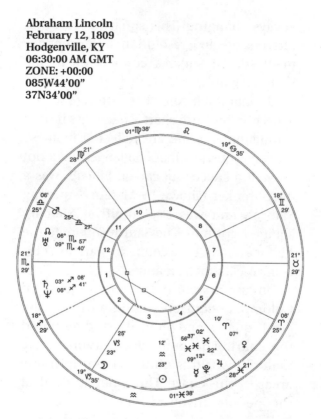

Geocentric
Tropical
Koch Houses

Figure 7. Abraham Lincoln's Natal Chart.

133

always changing. This square is one that often results in a resolution of the energies involved. All squares connect us to the material world.

Abraham Lincoln has strong square aspects in his birth chart. Challenges he met throughout his life are reflected in these aspects, yet show that challenges need not prevent a successful career. Lincoln was a deep thinker (shown by Mercury squaring Saturn), and was also intuitive (Mercury square Neptune). The Saturn square to the Midheaven may account in part for Lincoln's melancholic manner.

On January 25, 1999, an earthquake in Colombia occurred at a time when powerful squares and oppositions dominated the chart. The outer devastation of the material world is quite evident in many areas of the chart. The inner turmoil of the people involved was extreme. For individuals with many squares and oppositions, there can be a struggle to integrate the numerous challenges into a working set of strategies and tactics that partake of the potent energy without leading to explosive outbursts.

Earthquake, Columbia
January 25, 1999
Armenia, COL
01:19:00 PM EST
ZONE: +05:00
075 W41'00"
04N31'00"

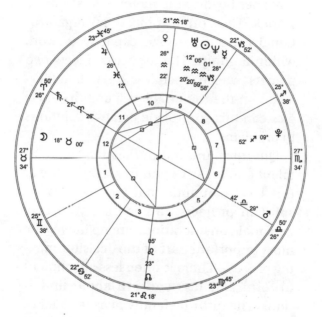

Geocentric
Tropical
Koch Houses

Figure 8. Earthquake in Columbia (1/25/99).

135

Quintile
Biquintile

Q BQ The quintile and biquintile aspects are indicative of a creative function that goes beyond the material or scientific worlds. They often indicate an organizational capacity, or the capacity to work within a group. The aspect connects two planets whose energies are well understood on the material level, and the energies can mix to provide creative solutions to problems.

Quintiles and biquintiles reflect latent talent and creative potential. Creativity at this level demands that you invest your spirit in projects, rather than your ego. Personal considerations are no longer the most important part of the decision-making process. There is often less attachment to form and less concern about limitations. The quintile family of aspects takes the energy of the planets involved, adds experience to the formula, and unifies intellect, emotion, and experience into one creative process.

Marilyn Monroe's chart has four quintiles and two biquintiles. Her acting career was reflected in these indicators of talent. She could use the energies of six different planets to achieve the expression of a role. In some areas she achieved striking success; in others she was surely unable to manifest her full range of talent.

Sextile

The sextile aspect relates planets that occupy compatible elements: fire to air, or earth to water. The aspect animates the two planets and indicates opportunities to use their energies together. You are able to create something of value, using those energies.

Sextiles contain all that is needed to produce. What you need to do is notice the opportunity, make a solid decision to move forward, and take action. You will find that the less ego you bring to this process, the easier it becomes. Your decision will be more precisely tuned to your higher needs, and movement occurs of its own accord. You don't need to push with sextiles, you only need to say "yes."

Marilyn Monroe
June 1, 1926
Los Angeles, CA
09:30:00 AM PST
ZONE: +08:00
118W15'00"
34N03'00"

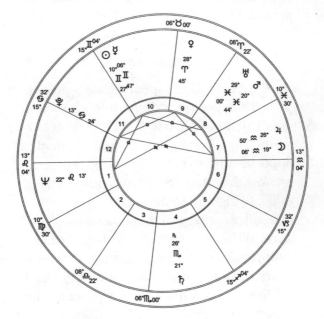

Geocentric
Tropical
Koch Houses

Figure 9. Marilyn Monroe's Natal Chart.

If you have a lot of sextiles in your birth chart, you will occasionally find that there are many opportunities at the same time. In such a situation the decision-making process becomes even more important. You will probably not be able to test every opportunity, and, therefore, must select on the information available. Communication is a necessary ingredient. You can share your thoughts with others and get feedback. The idea is to engage your mind, gather information, and then move forward.

Bill Clinton is surely plagued by his sextiles nearly as much as he benefits from them. Mercury sextiles Mars, Venus, Neptune, and the Ascendant. The Sun sextiles Jupiter on one side and Uranus on the other. While he has taken advantage of his opportunities, and risen to become the President of the United States, he has also fallen into the trap of saying "yes" to other opportunities that have led to financial and personal scandals. This is a good example of the fact that good judgment must be exercised in acting upon your opportunities.

Bill Clinton
August 19, 1946
Hope, AR
08:51:00 AM CST
ZONE: +06:00
093W35'00"
33N40'00"

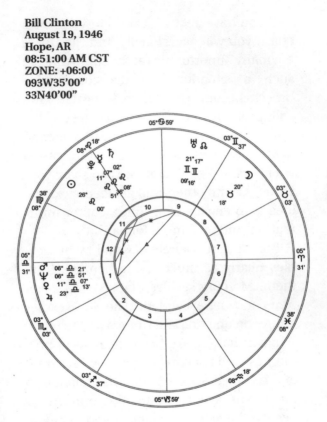

Geocentric
Tropical
Koch Houses

Figure 10. Bill Clinton's Natal Chart.

Semi-Square
Sesqui-Square

The semi-square and sesqui-square aspects are "internal" in the sense that you feel their energy, but the effect may not be evident to other people. The feelings range from irritation and insecurity to agitation, all of which are somewhat counterproductive. The creative potential lies in your ability to use the tension or stress as a barometer to measure the reality of a situation.

These aspects provide one way to stimulate your psychic or intuitive awareness. When the tension become noticeable to you, take the time to sit calmly and reflect on the feeling. Allow your mind to get "inside" the feeling—let it speak to you. Whatever thoughts arise as you sit, consider them in relation to your social life, your work, and your family. You may be surprised how clear the answers become when you listen to your own internal tension.

Semi-Sextile
Quincunx

These two aspects are indicators of growth and adjustment. Both of these conditions can be somewhat painful. They are not easy to control, and they tend to compel us to change whether we want to or not. The change is often accompanied by a realization about the self that you are unwilling to accept, at least at first. Both aspects may demand a lot of energy in dealing with those areas of your life.

The semi-sextile seems to bring growth through pain. We learn through this aspect to appreciate some aspect of our lives, but the flower of appreciation sometimes has thorns. The quincunx brings expansion that requires adjustment. You learn a lot about yourself and how to handle problems through this aspect. The quincunx is sometimes active at the time of an illness. This is because the body is fighting to expand its healing potential to ward off the illness or to repair physical damage.

For both the semi-sextile and the quin-cunx, you can think of one planet as the question and the other as the answer. One presents the area where growth or expansion is needed, and the other presents the method through which the adjustment can occur.

The Mayan calendar has predicted the end of the current cycle in December of 2012. The chart for this date contains a pattern of exact semi-sextiles and quincunxes, and suggests a global demand for growth and adjustment. Power and responsibility go hand in hand with justice and sound judgment. Growth will involve social systems and personal ideas and ideals. Change is a definite outcome of the configuration.

Summary

As you begin to consider aspects in your chart, you will look at them one at a time and try to understand their energy. It is very important to remember that no single aspect stands by itself. You will find that some aspects ring true—you understand exactly what the energies are doing. Other

End of Mayan Cycle
December 21, 2012
Cancún, MEX
09:30:00 PM CST
ZONE: +06:00
086W46'00"
21N05'00"

Geocentric
Tropical
Koch Houses

*Figure 11. End of Mayan Cycle
(12/21/2012).*

144

aspects will seem foreign, or simply meaningless. As you study each aspect, make a list or catalog of the possible meanings. You will begin to see a pattern of possibilities. When several aspects express similar energies, you have found an area of concentration that you can match to your experience. The occasional aspect that does not fit into such a pattern may add some zip to your life on occasion, but does not reflect a major part of your character.

It is also true that if you have many of one aspect, you will tend to think and act according to that aspect's style. The style of the sextile is to choose opportunities; the style of the square is to respond to the material world; the style of the opposition is to gain awareness; and the style of the conjunction is to experience beginnings and endings.

Aspects that are close to exact tend to have more impact than ones that are less precise. This is like tuning your radio: you get the strongest signal when you are tuned to the exact frequency. If you have several sextiles, for example, the one closest to exactly sixty degrees may express more often and more powerfully than the others may.

Finally, each aspect has an effect in the external environment as well as an internal, psychological effect. Often we tend to focus our attention on things outside ourselves because we are trying to make something happen in the environment. You will want to consider the impact on yourself of actions and events. The opportunity indicated by a sextile may at first seem to exist in the external world, but acting on that opportunity will have an internal effect as well. When you consider the mental, emotional, or spiritual impact of your actions, you will find you maintain your balance much better.

Chapter Nine

Transits and Progressions

Just as your birth chart shows where the planets were when you were born, at any moment another chart can be created. The planets in a chart for a particular moment are called *transits*. As the planets move through the zodiac, they interact with each other and they relate to the birth chart using the aspects that were described earlier.

Another popular kind of chart is called *progressions*. The planets in this chart are moved forward one day for each year of life. They reflect a different time scale—they move very slowly compared to the actual motion of the planets. Progressions show how you will respond to a larger cycle of activity, and progressed aspects are in effect for much longer time periods than transits.

The three charts are combined to forecast trends of activity and to pinpoint likely times when certain events may occur. Both progressions and transits are used to indicate action points in time, based on the potential in your birth chart. They show how the players in life's drama will interact with each other over time, based on individual potential as indicated in the birth chart. The house where a transiting planet is found indicates how its energy can be most easily expressed, just as the house in the birth chart shows the area of life where particular influences will be found.

It is important to remember that your birth potential determines the likelihood of events in your life. Each day there are easy or difficult transits, but they only affect you if they connect with your birth chart in some way. Today the planets may look good for an accident, but you will not have one if your birth chart doesn't show it. The same is true for winning the lottery—luck must be indicated in your birth chart as well as in today's planets.

Each planet indicates that a particular kind of energy is available in specific areas of your life, and the aspects formed to birth planets show times when that energy will be more active. The following descriptions of the planets relate to how they act in the day-to-day drama of life. You can get an idea of each transit by looking at the meaning of the planet and the sign it now occupies. Read the sections about the planet and the sign, and notice how they combine in a different way from your birth chart.

The Sun

The Sun brings light to the area of the chart it occupies. It focuses life energy there. You may be born with the Sun in Capricorn, a grounded, ambitious earth sign. As the Sun progresses into Aquarius, Pisces, and Aries during your life, you will find that the focus of your life changes, absorbing the qualities of those signs, and carrying that experience forward.

The daily positions of the planets are similar. As a Capricorn you may resonate to the energy of winter, but when the Sun is in Leo, you feel its light and warmth in a different way. When the Sun aspects a birth planet, that planet is in the spotlight. The "feel" of the spotlight depends on the aspect between the Sun and the birth planet.

Because the Sun moves rapidly through the signs, the progressions are more striking indicators of psychological and environmental forces. Progressions may indicate the entrance of a male into the picture. You may feel more determined and courageous, or possibly more "alive" in some way. Your sense of personal significance undergoes inspection when the progressed Sun forms aspects. Sun aspects affect your sense of self-esteem or conscientiousness, and often you can take pride in what you have accomplished after the aspect is past.

The Sun governs the heart and the spine. Progressed aspects can bring physical or emotional stress to these parts of the body. You may feel heartsick, or feel that you are carrying a heavy burden. Conversely, the Sun's aspects often bring the feeling of strength and vitality, uplifting the spirit and the body.

The Moon

)The Moon's position indicates the emotional tone of the moment. The Full Moon, for example, causes changes in the physical function of the body and in our emotional response to those changes. The Moon's sign indicates that specific unconscious information may be more readily available to us, filtered through the sign so that it has a specific tone. The Moon moves even faster than the Sun through the zodiac. Thus the phases of the Moon may have more significance than the daily positions. However, some people are very sensitive to the movement of the Moon—they feel the sifting of the tides within themselves each day. The Moon moves through an entire sign in a little over two days, so its effects are short-lived. However, the Moon sometimes acts as a trigger for the transit of a slower-moving planet. In a detailed analysis of a time period, the aspects the Moon makes can tell an intriguing story of the unfolding of events.

Progressions of the Moon may indicate the entrance of a female into your life, or the influence of a female on your activities. They can indicate times when your emotions are disrupted. You may find that thoughts concerning women, your home, and children fill your time. You find that activities involve many people and ordinary activities or commodities.

Health issues revolve around the stomach, mental complaints, the eyes, and the ears. Your stomach may become the barometer of your feelings under progressed Moon aspects. You may notice changes in perception, such as changes in the ability to discern colors or sounds. Musical tastes may change during lunar progressions.

Mercury

☿ Just as the god Mercury was the messenger of the other gods, so the planet Mercury is an indicator of communication. Mercury moves faster than any other planet, so here again the influence is transitory. In addition, the planet Mercury tends to take on the character of the planet it is aspecting, so you can usually say that there is some communication concerning the other planet's nature. A third factor is that Mercury (and the rest of the planets) appears to go backward in the sky. Mercury does this three times a year. During those periods you often have a chance to review your actions and revise your plans.

Mercury often indicates what you were thinking about. Again, the nature of the other planet describes the nature of the thoughts. For example, Mars relates to energy. A Mercury/Mars aspect might indicate thoughts about physical activity, or a telephone call about some plans. The communication can occur quickly, or there may be an argumentative quality to it. Some kind of exchange is always part of the equation.

Progressed Mercury can bring you into prolonged contact with the written word, telephone or telegraph, and all forms of communication. You may find your capacity for study changes dramatically.

Health issues include a tendency to nervousness, hay fever or asthma (if you are susceptible), intense mental activity, and bowel complaints. All of these are related to your stress level is some way, and Mercury's aspects point to the kind of person or situation that is causing the stress. Clearer communication in that area helps to relieve all sorts of mental and physical symptoms.

Venus

♀ Venus brings thoughts of love and harmony into the equation. It may indicate a physical or sexual attraction—Venus can act almost like a magnet drawing you together with another person or an object, or into a social situation. The other person may be an artist or entertainer, or perhaps a younger female.

Venus in a transiting aspect can indicate a deepening of feeling, or even the beginning of love. Venus moves fairly quickly, so it indicates a momentary feeling, one that will pass within a day or so. However, when a slower transiting planet forms an aspect with your birth Venus, this can indicate the appearance or reunion with an individual who is described by the transiting planet—a person who can become a strong love interest: if Mars, perhaps the transit indicates a strong, energetic person; if Jupiter, someone tall or large; if Saturn, someone much older or younger; if Uranus, a person who could easily become the love of your life; if Neptune, a mystical type; or, if Pluto, a person who has an overpowering effect on you, or a fanatical sort of person.

Progressed Venus can attract like a magnet. You may see more flowers and candy from your significant other! You may also have greater interest in clothing and jewelry, and your tastes in food may shift. Social events take on greater significance when Venus is active.

Venus governs the kidneys, skin, veins, thyroid, and female reproductive organs. Progressed Venus can indicate the onset of problems in these areas. Venus also is involved in sexually transmitted diseases. Not every Venus aspect brings trouble in these areas, but when you have an aspect, it is wise to moderate your diet and activities, or to take steps to protect yourself from disease.

Mars

♂ The transit of Mars indicates a part of your life where energy is being directed. It can feel like you have more physical energy to work and play. It can also feel like there is much more mental, emotional, or spiritual energy available. You will perhaps feel greater determination to accomplish what you need to do. It is important not to become stubborn in your desire to make progress, but rather to use the excitement and enthusiasm wisely. This is sometimes easy to say and more difficult to accomplish.

You may find that you are surrounded with people who express the energy of Mars clearly. They may include athletes or people interested in sports, people in the military or who have a military bearing, surgeons, doctors, and other people who may treat injuries, or possibly people who enjoy a vigorous conversation or argument.

As you use your energy, you may feel alternating periods of weakness or lack of energy. It is important to allow time for rest when Mars is present. If you become exhausted, you may be careless and cause accidents or injury to yourself or others.

Remember, Mars energy is the kind you use to do ordinary things; it fuels the body as well as your car. When Mars is active, expect to see and feel more energy in every area of your life, but particularly where the aspected planet is active. If Mars aspects the Sun, you will feel personally energized; if in aspect with the Moon, you may have very active dreams and imagination; with Mercury, your communications will be fast and vigorous; with Venus, there may be powerful sexual energy around you; with Mars, you get a chance to evaluate your life's course regarding how you use energy in general; with Jupiter, you may feel like a balloon expanding near the bursting point; with Saturn, inhibited energy, endurance, or resistance; with Uranus, sudden, surprising action; with Neptune, weakness or dissatisfaction; or, with Pluto, compulsive actions or a feeling of great power and confidence.

Jupiter

When Jupiter transits or progresses to form aspects, there will be expansion. Jupiter brings hopefulness, sociability, and harmony to the other planet. There is activity along philosophical or philanthropic lines. Generally, Jupiter reflects a sense of benevolence in the area of the other planet.

Sometimes, if Jupiter indicates a too-rapid expansion, there can be loss after the expansion, or poor judgment, or other problems indicates by the aspect and the nature of the other planet. Still, the overall feeling of Jupiter is of hope, good will, and generosity.

In the environment, Jupiter is connected to merchandise, bankers, and professional people. Thus it is often involved at times when big business or career changes occur. Jupiter greases the wheels of commerce by providing the optimism to encourage taking a risk. The church or clergy may be involved when Jupiter transits your chart.

Health indications of Jupiter transits include overabundance in general. This can involve weight gain through over-indulgence in food. In more extreme cases it can indicate changes in the function of liver, pancreas, and other glands, often associated with excessive consumption of alcohol, sugars, and fats, leading to problems associated with these organs. While tumors are related to Saturn, their abnormal growth is related to Jupiter.

Saturn

♄ When Saturn is strongly involved in progressions and transits, there is a tendency to concentrate and draw into yourself. You may find that you are only able to focus on one thing at a time, when you usually can keep many things balanced. There is a sense of heavy responsibility reflected in Saturn transits. You may feel that you have the weight of Saturn on your shoulders or back. There is likely to be more work, or work of a more intense, concentrated nature.

Financially such a contraction or limitation may be felt as a financial loss. Even if you don't lose property, you may feel deprived or insecure. Thus your thoughts make turn to safety issues, secrets, or worry. You may want to acquire everything you need immediately, instead of pacing your spending. In this way the very feeling of lack depletes your financial reserves.

Saturn relates to structure. It governs bones, skin, teeth, and hair. Saturnian health issues relate to deficiencies of various kinds. If there is not enough water, your digestive tract becomes sluggish, for example. Without enough vitamins and other nutrients, the bones become weak, or the hair lacks luster and strength. Saturn also indicates the chronic progress or development of disease. On the psychological level, you may feel the aspects of Saturn to its birth location very strongly. The Saturn returns at around ages twenty-eight and fifty-six may bring prominent conclusions to entire phases of life.

On the environmental level, Saturn governs utilities, minerals, grain, building materials, mines, real estate, and more. The organizational structure and policies of corporations are reflected by Saturn, while the day-to-day process of transacting

business is related to Jupiter, and communications themselves relate to Mercury.

It is helpful to remember that the struc-
turing or restructuring indicated by a Saturn transit does not in itself bring limitation or restriction. We need structure to
function comfortably. If you feel isolated,
you can reach out to someone else, remov-
ing the perceived barrier.

Uranus

Uranus moves very slowly by progression and by transit. Yet its aspects
indicate sudden, even revolutionary
change. There will be a strong desire for
independence and enthusiasm for all
things new and different in your life.

You may find that your intuitive abilities
are stronger, or that they emerge and
develop more fully during Uranus transits.
This planet reflects the capacity to relate
today's events to the future, and to guide
your life skillfully based on your inner
sense of direction. This is liberating for the
soul but can cause upsets in your daily life

if you allow your impulses to carry you too far too fast.

Uranus often indicates that other people are directly involved in events that affect you deeply. You may not be able to forecast who these people will be—they may remain unknown to you, too. Uranus governs inventions, from the automobile to electricity, from computers to all types of mechanical devices. It also governs antiques. This seems strange at first, but old objects are often imbued with the psychic vibrations that stimulate intuition. Professions such as astrology and psychology use the intuitive sense to help clients.

Health indications include paralysis, nervous disorders, and arthritis. The very planet that can indicate sudden movement or change also governs severe limitation of movement. Diseases with a sudden onset, like appendicitis, are related to this planet.

The overall quality is equilibrium. Uranus' energy serves to bring us back into balance. The more out of balance we are, the more striking the effect of a Uranus transit. When we are on track intuitively we feel less drama when Uranus aspects hit.

Uranus is a good timer of events—many times the event happens exactly when Uranus forms the exact aspect. Don't look for events before that time!

Neptune

Neptune transits bring glamour into your life. This can mean dressed-up, fantasy-related activities, or the deception of the stage magician. There is often a sense of protection that accompanies the feeling of unreality. Thus danger is some-times a factor. You, may find yourself involved with unusual people and weird events. Yet you may also find that your psychic senses are tuned precisely.

Any progression or transit increases the imagination and sensitivity to people around you. Behavior is influenced by wishful thinking or fantasy. Scheming may develop into a pattern of action and can be detrimental to your work, as your focus on a promotion or other goal can detract from your daily accomplishments.

In your environment, you may encounter the promoter, the confidence man, and the individual who plots and schemes. You come into contact with movie stars, mystics, and psychic energy. A profit sharing venture may be presented to you.

Health issues relating the Neptune include negative attitudes, bacterial infection, and oversensitivity in the psychic area. There is a possibility of poisoning or allergic response. Thus when you have Neptune aspects you need to take care to flush the system with enough water each day, and to maintain a clean environment. At the same time your psychic senses can provide what you need to protect your health in the form of messages or dreams.

In general, the receptivity of Neptune provides the path to sympathy and understanding of other people. When you are very open to it, the energy can become confused, the psychic messages vague, and you may feel you are less capable of effective planning. It may help to logically consider what you are focused on and then use the Neptunian path of devotion to stick to the goals you have set. When your devotion is focused, it is less likely that others can derail your efforts.

Pluto

Strong Pluto aspects by transit or progression indicate the influence of groups or the possibility of coercion. You may feel that any willingness to cooperate on your part opens you to being pushed—the old "give an inch, take a mile" response. Of course it is possible that you will try to take the mile yourself! The forces at work are subtle but powerful. You can benefit from careful analysis of situations. Withhold your decision until you have had time to think it through logically. Most decisions can be put off for one day without harm. Statistical analysis of a problem may be helpful. Gathering data helps to quantify the problem and point to appropriate choices.

The people in your environment who want to influence your decisions may range from highly developed spiritual beings to people on the wrong side of the law. Radio and television may play an active role in your life when Pluto is active. You may be close to drastic events that bring sweeping change, often for the better.

Health issues include allergies and hay fever. Bees and bee pollen may figure in your treatments of allergies. There may be an invasion of other organisms, such as a virus, or there may be an injury such as a puncture wound. When Pluto and, indeed, any of the outer planets, are active, you will want to be careful to focus on what you are doing and try not to let your mind wander from the task.

In general, Pluto transits bring you into contact with power. You may feel alternately powerful in yourself and pushed or oppressed because of the power others exert. You have the capacity to reach deep into the collective mind for strength, and your ability to regenerate after an injury or illness is very strong. Maintaining balance can be a challenge, but keeping your own center or regaining it will become easier as you go through the transit. Pluto brings change with no going back. When you have Pluto strong in your chart, you can be the trendsetter and an effective instrument of positive change. Pluto cleanses and revitalizes. ESP also can be an active source of data. Don't expect peace and quiet.

Chapter Ten

Putting It All Together: More Questions and Answers

What is the meaning of the shapes in the center of my chart?

The shapes drawn in the center of the chart are patterns formed by connecting any two planets that form an aspect. The lines help to identify patterns of energy. When they form a triangle, square, or other figures, they show where the flow is continuous, and therefore where you can develop greater strength or talent.

What is the significance of the planets that are bunched together in my chart?

When planets are close together, it concentrates the energies. It does not mean that other areas of your life are empty. Instead, it indicates that your life is very focused, and that the "empty" areas depend on the areas where the focus is found. Thus an empty Fifth House does not mean you will not have children. It means that the children in your life are an outgrowth of expression in some other area.

How long does it take to really learn astrology?

You can learn enough to be conversant about astrology in a short time, depending on how concentrated your studies are. To become proficient enough to call yourself a professional can take several years. Remember, you can earn a master's degree in most subjects in one and a half to two years of full-time study and practice, or you can study the subject throughout your life as a more leisurely pace. Astrology is about the same.

Where can I find some books? I'm just a beginner (I know some stuff), but I don't have a new age bookstore close to me.

You can request a Llewellyn catalog of astrology books. It is free, and tells a bit about the content of each title. Beginner's books generally focus on one subject, such as planets, or the title will indicate they are beginning-level books. The description of the titles should help to determine if they are at your level. Even very advanced books will have something to offer to the beginner, but it is a lot easier to start at the beginning and work up to them.

Is there such a thing as a "bad chart" or being born under a "bad sign?"

No. Some writers have allowed their personal prejudices to creep into their work, but the signs are equal, if very different expressions of energy. It is true that what is difficult for one person is merely "life" for another. It is also true that some periods of time are more challenging than others. Astrology helps to see the flow of energy in your life and provide insight into the challenges and their solutions.

Do the planets really dictate my actions?

No. They provide a picture—a reflection—of your being. The birth chart reflects the larger universe at the time you were born, and thus provides a map of energy to which you can respond directly. The transits are the map of the planets at a given moment. Their relationship to your birth chart shows how your own energy relates to the energy of the present moment. This helps you to understand what you are thinking and feeling—it gives you something outside yourself to relate to.

How can I get information about my birth chart? My romantic life? My career? What's happening right now?

Llewellyn offers an array of astrological services. They include expansive interpretations of your chart, comparisons of your chart to your significant other's chart, or explanations about the current transits. See the appendix for a description of each of the reports, its purpose, and value.

Summary

Astrology is a tool for growth and change that is based on a solid history of experience. It does not depend on psychic ability and is therefore different from other divination techniques. It provides a new "alphabet" of factors that weave together into a wonderful language of life, with cyclical flows and turnings.

Detailed understanding of your astrological chart provides helpful information about your natural potential, and also indicates the ups and downs you encounter on your path. But you are not a mere passenger! Astrology does not replace common sense and intelligence. Rather, it can provide the information you need to make wise choices. It puts you in the driver's seat, with a map of the territory and all the fuel you need for a successful tour.

Appendix

Tools and Resources

Now that you've finished your tour of the basics behind the ancient art of astrology, you are probably anxious to try it all out! Llewellyn takes pride in having been a major force in promoting astrology for nearly a century. As such, we have a wealth of books, annuals, and services at your disposal. In the following pages, you will find a comprehensive array of chart services that cover virtually every aspect of life. The whole purpose of astrology is to give you a way to improve your life and the lives of others. Now that you're ready, start putting astrology to work today!

Start off right with a *Professional Natal Chart.*

If you are a student or professional astrologer and prefer to do your own interpretations, you need to be sure you are starting with an accurate and detailed birth chart. The Professional Natal Chart is generated by Matrix Software's best-selling WinStar 2.0 software. It is loaded with information, including a chart wheel, aspects, declinations, nodes, major asteroids, and more. (Tropical zodiac/ Placidus houses, unless specified otherwise.)
APS03-119 $5.00

Gain a deeper understanding with an *Astro*Talk Advanced Natal Report.*

Without a doubt, this is one of the most thorough interpretations of your birth chart you will ever read. Written in plain English by world-famous astrologer Michael Erlewine, these detailed descriptions of the unique effects of the planets on your character and life will amaze and enlighten you. Included in this thirty-plus page report are: your Rising Sign; your planets' signs and aspects; your challenges and abilities; your major life periods; your burn rate; your soul type; your current influences; your chart's houses; and more. See how your birth chart contains the keys to self-understanding.
APS03-525 $30.00

Everything you've always wanted to know about yourself but were afraid to ask with *Heaven Knows What.*

Get your personality and destiny interpreted by the man most modern astrologers learned their art from. This report contains a classic interpretation of your birth chart and a look at upcoming events, as presented by the time-honored master of the astrological arts, Grant Lewi. Clear and concise, these descriptions of the influences of the planets on your inner self go light-years beyond the one-size-fits-all descriptions found in magazines and popular astrology books. Also included is a look at your year ahead, as laid out in the patterns of the stars and planets.

APS03-532 $30.00

Get the feminine perspective with *Woman to Woman.*

Finally, astrology from a feminine point of view! World-renowned astrologer Gloria Star brings her special style and insight to this detailed look into the mind, soul, and spirit of the modern female. This report will show you the truth about yourself in a way that only another woman could understand. Read about: your projection of your real self; meeting the world on your terms; and power issues of sex, money, and control.

APS03-531 $30.00

Your map to the future is a *TimeLine Transit/Progression Forecast.*

Love, money, health—everybody wants to know what lies ahead, and this report will keep you one-up on your future. The *TimeLine* forecast is invaluable for seizing opportunities and timing your moves. This astrological report is completely tailored to you—a unique individual with a unique relation to the cosmos. Reports begin the first day of the month you specify.

APS03-526	3-month report	$12.00
APS03-527	6-month report	$20.00
APS03-528	12-month report	$30.00

Stop looking for love in all the wrong places with *Friends and Lovers.*

Why can't we all just get along? Well, sometimes we can and sometimes we can't, and astrology can shed a lot of light on what makes the difference when you start with a custom-made report like *Friends and Lovers.* Go way beyond "does Capricorn get along with Sagittarius?" Find out how you relate to others, and whether you are really compatible with your current or potential lover, spouse, friend, or business partner! This service includes planetary placements for both people, so send birth data for both and specify "friends" or "lovers."

APS03-529 $20.00

Find out if you and your lover are truly matched with *Sympaticos.*

You have a chart, and your love partner has a chart, but did you know that your relationship has a chart, too? It does—the Composite Chart—a blend of the birth charts of two people, and the method behind this amazingly insightful new report. With *Sympaticos*, you will find out the real secrets of what exists between you, and the essence of what you can do and be together. Be sure to include birth data for both people.

APS03-533 $20.00

Give your child a jump on life with *Child*Star.*

We all want the best for our children, and a large part of that comes from understanding who they are and where their latent talents and challenges lie. Every parent knows that each child enters the world with a unique, distinct personality, and astrology can reveal the forces behind that fresh new face. Written by an astrologer who is also a Montessori© instructor, *Child*Star* is an astrological look at your child's inner world through a skillful interpretation of his or her unique birth chart, and is as relevant for teens as it is for newborns. Specify your child's sex.

APS03-530 $20.00

Now you can take this job and love it with *Opportunities*.

Your career is more than just a job—it's where the real you meets the real world. If you want to know just what the best fit might be, you need this enlightening and detailed report. Your unique talents are needed by someone out there, and by fulfilling that need you will not only be contributing to the world, but to your soul's growth as well. With the right livelihood, you could actually begin to look forward to Mondays!

APS03-534   **$20.00**

Astrological Services Order Form

Report name and number:

_____

Provide the following data on all persons receiving a report:
1st Person's Full Name, including current middle & last name(s):

_____

Birthplace (city, county, state, country):

_____

_____

Birthtime:_____ a.m. p.m. (please circle)

Month:_____ Day:_____ Year:_____

2nd Person's Full Name (if ordering for more than one person):

_____

Birthplace (city, county, state, country):

_____

_____

Birthtime:_____ a.m. p.m. (please circle)

Month:_____ Day:_____ Year:_____

Billing Information

Name:_____

Address:_____

City:_____

State/Zip: _____ Country:_____

Day phone:_____

Make check or money order payable to Llewellyn Publications, or charge it!

Circle one: Visa MasterCard American Express

Acct. No. _____

Exp. Date _____

Cardholder Signature

_____

☐ Yes! Send me my free copy of New Worlds!

Mail this form and payment to:

Llewellyn's Computerized Astrological Services
P.O. Box 64383, Dept. K-146-5 • St. Paul, MN 55164-0383

Allow 4-6 weeks for delivery.